HOMECOMINGS: AN ODYSSEY

AN UNEXPECTED JOURNEY IN LIFE

A MEMOIR BY

Z.Z. GOLDBERG

Homecomings: An Odyssey
An Unexpected Journey in Life

Copyright 2016 by Z.Z. Goldberg
Email: Modiinsg@gmail.com
Blog: Homecomings: An Odyssey

First Edition 2017
Printed: Self Published by Amazon

Cover design: Sidra Collins
Edited by: Mitchell Chanelis

ISBN 13-978-1545412701

1. Religious aspects. 2. Memoirs. 3. Odyssey 4. Mental Health. 5. Nostalgia

DEDICATIONS

This memoir was written in dedication to my mother and father...Although I was physiologically, physically and emotionally mistreated by my mother, I felt that it was one way that I could honor her by dedicating this work of non-fiction to her.. A way to heal myself and forgive and above all....learn so many lessons from her mistakes and the mistakes that I made.

The struggle I had for so many years, was trying to understand how to put these true events down in writing, worried that I wouldn't be honoring my mother. It's taken most of my life time, but I have come to realize that there's a difference between honoring one's parents and loving them. I'm being honest with myself in saying that: No, I didn't love my mother...I felt as if I was in a nightmare and always wanted to escape her clutches. I was sad when she died and felt sorry for her tortured life.

This work is also dedicated to my three daughters: Neima, Sidra and Gema, who have been many things to me in life but above all - Blessings.

They have heard my stories over the years but now they can keep them and share with their children. I love you girls beyond words.

To my beautiful Grandma Molly, whose Shabbat candles sparked the light for me and to my lovely Aunt Martha, who endured a hard life but got to see a promise fulfilled and of course to my mother, Frances Goldberg, whose soul, I hope has found rest and peace that she was so desperately searching for in this life.

ACKNOWLEDGEMENTS:

The process of writing this work has taken over 15 yrs. Because life tends to take over and it got pushed on the back burner of real life events. But I want to acknowledge and thank the many people along my journey, for giving me the push and encouragement that I've needed over the years to make this project a reality: All my siblings...Mitchell my oldest brother whose gifted talent was able to edit this manuscript and who gave me incredible enthusiasm to move forward, Warren my youngest brother who has been such a support emotionally and physically at just the right times, when he was there for me. And of course, my sister Mickey (Malda, Linda), who was the inspiration and reason for sharing these life stories with the world.

To my daughters and to my grandchildren: Ainsley, Aryeh, Ayala, Emily and Dominic.

To my many relatives, friends, neighbors and employers who have taught me valuable life lessons and who have been along for various parts of the journey with me: Rabbi Aaron, Marilyn, Debby, Leslie, Monik, Sarah, Chaya, Miri, Racheli, Linda, Roni, Steve, Bully, Bill, all my EX's (my Ex-Files) and ex mother-in-law's (Wanda, Ruby and Shirley) who were truly my friends.

To my Creator who continues to sustain me throughout my life and has given me many gifts, blessings, creativity and talents and brought me to such a time as this.

FAMILY

After fifty-six years of sworn family secrets and cover-ups, fruitless searches, and separation, in a few hours I would meet the sister I never knew. We would spend the next four days in Manhattan finding out all we could about each other, and about our new-found respective families. I had as yet unanswered questions swirling through my brain: Which of her three siblings would she most resemble? What if we don't like each other? Why did our mother give her away and not us? How would we make up for fifty-six years of separation in under a week? What if our kids don't get along? What if we don't relate to each other as sisters? If I tell her everything I know about our mother will it shatter her image of who she thinks our mother was? The future viability of our long-lost relationship was hanging in the balance.

My anxieties would be calmed in good time; the most intriguing question of the moment, though, was why did we at last and now find each other? I'd always believed that nothing happens by chance; and then in my mid-fifties it seemed that the chance of a lifetime had come to find and redeem someone and something which had been lost.

Each of us, two girls out of four siblings, had yearned to fill an unnamable, aching void. My sister's search had begun twenty-six years earlier and mine twelve years later. We'd both received the shocking news of family dislocation through arguments with our respective mothers, however in profoundly dissimilar circumstances: Malda had grown up in the limelight of the Copacabana night club in its heyday; with a wealthy celebrity father and all the glamorous trappings: there was a house full of servants, fine clothes, and almost anything else a young girl would want. I had been raised in scarcity, was shuffled back and forth from orphanages to foster homes and back again to a troubled and emotionally unstable mother. We had moved frequently from one welfare-subsidized apartment to another. While Malda, after discovering, from her ex-Ziegfeld Follies showgirl mother, that she'd been adopted, developed a romantic, fairy tale longing for a lost mother who would come and rescue the poor little rich girl from her in-name-only family. Fabulously ensconced in a sixteen-room apartment on Fifth Avenue overlooking Central Park, life seemed picture perfect to anyone who thought they knew our missing sister. Our mother Frances, though, could liberate neither herself nor the three children who remained with her, much less the girl who got away. Oddly, we were to discover that what we did have in common were lives of insufficient love.

STORIES

My older brother Mitchell and I were driving to New York City from Boston. It was early June 2001. In just a few hours the much-anticipated family reunion would take place on the upper West Side of Manhattan at the apartment of Malda's oldest daughter, Jama. We wanted to be prepared. What better way than to regale ourselves with family stories?

Three years after the Great War ended in 1918 another war began: the life of our mother Frances Goldberg. Frances was born on June 20, 1921 in Brooklyn, New York to Molly (Esther Malka Fensterscheib) and Max (Aaron Mandel) Goldberg. Molly and Max had married in 1908 with financial help from Grandma Molly's aunt & uncle the Saltzmans.

Esther Malka and her family of seven (all siblings) had emigrated to the New World from Austrian Poland. They'd washed up poor at Ellis Island during the second

 great wave of European immigration which had begun in the late 1800s. Max's family hailed from Russian Poland. Frances was the youngest of their three children. Louis was the first-born and Martha (Margaret) followed him six years later. The older two were typical, standard issue kids to their immigrant Jewish parents. It was the Roaring Twenties, but life didn't roar much for the Goldbergs. They couldn't

afford much and, like most immigrant families of the day, struggled to make ends meet. Something, though, was not run of the mill with our little mother-to-be. Frances was pretty, extroverted, and flamboyant; not what grandma Molly expected or accepted from her little girl. Grandpa Max, though, favored her and showered his love onto the cute, feisty, and boisterous baby. She was protected when daddy was around. Little Francie could do no wrong in his eyes; daddy was her guardian angel. Molly and Martha were rivals and jealous; they took any opportunity to exact retribution. Frances could do no right in their eyes. Uncle Louie was out of the house and married by the time our mother-to-be reached the age of eleven.

Max was a prankster and was especially fond of teasing his straight-laced wife. He'd delight in tricking Molly with a joke or prank. Grandpa was a barber and his shop was downstairs from the apartment at 1947 Bergen Street. Once he had Martha go upstairs and report to him Molly's reaction when she saw the conspicuously placed rubber dog poop he'd placed on the carpet. She predictably saw the rubber dropping and was predictably furious convinced, Foo Foo, their dog had done the dirty deed. Max would laugh, as he had many times before; chalking up yet another victory in the daily quest to get his wife good. Francie spent a lot of time in the barber shop watching her dad give neighborhood kids, boys and girls alike, Buster Brown haircuts. He would call up to Molly every day and have her send down his lunch of coffee and eggs; one of the Goldberg kids would take down the eggs. Molly, though, had a special way of sending down the coffee - in a can, out the window, lowered by rope since the apartment was two stories up.

Max was not a religious man and didn't attend the local Synagogue. Molly, though, religiously attended Synagogue during the High Holy Days; and every Friday night at sundown she would, without fail, light Sabbath candles; and religiously each week Martha would go to the Synagogue with two dollars from her mother for charity. Grandpa Max, contrarily, immensely enjoyed  attending evangelical Christian Tent Revival Meetings and would often bring along little Francie. The animated religious gatherings were highly entertaining to the Jewish barber from Brooklyn; the Tent Meetings were another world to him. The mostly black congregants would joyously sing, dance, and get wild in their worship. Grandpa Max made sure though that his little pal told no one, especially her mother, that she had accompanied him to the revival meetings. Grandpa Max, assured of secrecy, felt free to mimic for the inspiration and entertainment of his small family how the blacks would sing, shout, and roll in the aisles. He loved to demonstrate how the black folks got into it; throwing up his hands he'd wildly dance around the living room, everyone laughing at his antics and merry making.

Life in general, however, was far from entertaining for the Goldberg family. Catastrophe would overtake them on June 20th, 1930, Francie's ninth birthday. She and her daddy had planned something special to celebrate the day. Grandpa Max started shaving while his adoring little daughter looked on; she loved to watch him. Frances was mature for her age and already a maverick; she'd already amassed a full repertoire of theatrics only appreciated by her father. Almost finished shaving, Grandpa Max suddenly collapsed on the floor, dead from a massive heart attack. There her father lay before her. Life as she'd known it was over. The feisty kid's main defender was gone. Who would be there for her now? Molly had to cope with singlehandedly mothering two girls, a struggle in the best of times; Louie would be leaving home to get married and would soon start his own family. The Great Depression was rapidly advancing; there was little income aside from what her children might bring in.

The death of her beloved champion and protector overnight transformed Frances from her father's favorite into the small family's black sheep. Psychology as a discipline had barely emerged from the rarified confines of Freud's Vienna. There was no one willing, able, or available to care about or understand the trauma the young girl went through with the sudden and devastating loss of her father and closest ally. Molly had her own pain and fear to cope with. Sheer survival was the order of the day during the imminent downturn known as the

Great Depression. Martha would always be jealous that her father favored Francie. Louis, now the man of the family, was almost out of the house and increasingly focused on his impending marriage to Grace. Already poor, those remaining on Bergen Street had to face head on the economic abyss of the 1930s.

DEPRESSION

The exuberant, inflated prosperity of the 1920s was paralleled by the unprecedented, draconian enactment of Prohibition. Perhaps a well-intentioned policy intended to reduce the consumption of alcohol and alleviate the negative social consequences of pathological drunkenness, the medicine of Prohibition almost killed the patient; and certainly, didn't achieve its intended goals during the thirteen years it was in effect. Enforcement of Prohibition proved impossible. Time-honored habits and social customs which involved the consumption of alcohol collided with ideological and legislative roadblocks set up by social reformers. To the adventuresome, obstacles are meant to be surmounted; almost immediately upon its enactment Prohibition spawned the monster of organized crime which, perversely, eased passage through, without dismantling, the roadblocks. Widespread political corruption flourished along with bootlegging and the speakeasies.

In 1925, there were more than one hundred thousand speakeasies in New York City alone. Even though all the legal saloons had been shut down, it was easy to get a drink from an illegal speakeasy. They were located in basements and office buildings down almost any street and were open at all hours. Mobsters became heroes to Americans thirsting for freedom from the cant and hypocrisy of reformers. There was also the thrill of it, a wide scale social adventure bonding fellow citizen law breakers! Along with almost universal, flagrant violations of the despised law came the numerous gangs of organized crime. New York City had a hefty share of resident mobsters, but Chicago reigned supreme as the undisputed hub of organized crime. Brownsville in

Brooklyn, Goldberg central, was HQ for Murder, Inc. the most notorious of the Jewish mobs.

The 1930s in America were the era of the Great Depression - characterized by bread lines, Apple Annie, and almost no work. Around twenty five percent of the American workforce were out of a job. The Thirties were also the heyday of gloriously escapist song and dance Hollywood movies, and the palaces within which they were shown; usually in double bills with live floor shows to boot. Daily entertainment, though, for most families would be to gather around a large console radio in the middle of the living room and listen to an extraordinary array of music, comedy, and drama which would provide the basis for much early television programming in the 1950s, TV's golden age. There was Little Orphan Annie, and God Bless America (a popular tune by another Jewish New Yorker, Irving Berlin, which would become America's unofficial national anthem). The Empire State building took thirteen months to build and was completed in 1934. Pluto was discovered. After Prohibition was lifted in 1933 the night club era burst through its speakeasy bonds and came to resemble an explosion of fireworks across the midnight sky. Brooklyn was New York City's most populous borough with, including the Goldberg clan, over two million souls.

The Great Depression's effects on children were, of course, radically different from the impact on their parents. Kids often took on great responsibility at an earlier age than would later generations. Especially for immigrant families it was easier for kids, who were fluent in English and acculturated to American ways, to find work. Teenagers worked when their parents couldn't, a generational reversal of the traditional roles of provider and dependent.

Born in Brooklyn during the flapper era, Frances Goldberg came into her youth during the pre-World War II Depression years. In Louis' absence, Martha stepped in and assumed the role of breadwinner; she was ready, willing, and able to take primary responsibility for supporting the family. Frances continued to be Daddy's Little Girl although daddy was gone; it was much more fun for her, an extremely attractive and gregarious young

woman, to hang out with local mobsters and, eventually, frequent bars and night clubs.

Frances's fondest dream was to be in the theater and become an actress. She secretly enrolled in a local WPA (Works Progress Administration) acting class. Somehow Martha found out about her little sister's flirtation with the theater and, so the story goes, unexpectedly appeared as the budding

thespian was onstage practicing a scene. Shrieking that Frances was a whore, Martha dragged, by the hair, her horrified sister offstage. The end; finis; exit stage left! Night life became Frances's way of manifesting her aspiration and desire. The culturally dominant chord struck for the young then was, "have a good time"! Elaborate rags to riches, anyone-can-make-it, musicals such as, "Gold Diggers of 1933" and "42nd Street" fed Depression-era audiences what they craved - escape! Glamour was portrayed as the mark of success. Weekly salaries for average workers in the 1930s and early 40s were about twelve dollars. Frances figured out early on that her desired lifestyle required more than twelve bucks a week if she was to support herself and her mother too. Smoking by the age of twelve, at fifteen Frances started to drink.

At about age twelve Frances would earn money for the family by running numbers for the gangsters and bookies in Brownsville, a common way for neighborhood kids of a certain bent to earn cash. The young were in demand  because they could move more easily and evade police suspicion and surveillance. For Frances, it was a natural; she put herself out there, on a stage of sorts, taking risks and acting the part of an innocent kid. She was also earning money and admiration from the big guys. The extra cash, she hoped, would boost her standing with her mother and sister. Whatever attempts, though, the enterprising girl made to help support her widowed mother would be belittled by her older sister. Martha was in charge and fulfilled that role for many years.

Finances aside; when, according to Frances, she worked up the courage to tell her mother that at the age of twelve an uncle had raped her, Molly refused to accept her word and dismissed the account. Respectable people didn't talk about such things in those days; and a child's word could not be trusted especially when it came to such an accusation against an adult, one of Molly's brothers! After that any sense of truly belonging to the Goldbergs evaporated for Frances. The emotional security of family life began its decline with the sudden death of Max. Without her father around, general male attention would have to fill the bill; and she'd find solace and admiration from other men. Because of her beauty and budding, vibrant sexuality there was no shortage of male attention. Local mobsters and their hangers on became her substitute family. They possessed the requisite glamour of rebellion so appealing to youth, as well as the social ways and financial means to facilitate escape from her jail on Bergen Street.

At such a tender age, did Frances either understand or care that her eagerness to fulfill the desire of various men would ultimately not compensate for the lost love and protection she craved? In any case, she kept looking and not finding. Frances was seen as promiscuous; a humiliation to her mother and sister, 'good Jews' who maintained their respectability in the midst of financial difficulties.

The struggling Goldberg family would move to Brownsville in Brooklyn where Martha would marry her first husband. Martha and Nat lived upstairs from Molly and Frances's one bedroom apartment in the small building at 1815 Sterling Place. Martha emotionally struggled with her first and only child's birth. A physician's forceps damaged her son Mark's skull at delivery and marked him as retarded for the rest of his life. Frances had her own troubles and could offer little support to her older sister; and, as well, would continue to torment her mother with worry. Frances would regularly be out with her gang till all hours and sometimes wouldn't even come home at night. Molly would be frantic and go half-crazy trying to keep track of her rebellious daughter. Her youngest daughter loved to sit outside on the stoop in front of the building and talk into the wee hours of the night to guys and girlfriends. What could her daughter possibly be talking about until five or six in the morning? Frances would seize any opportunity to get dolled up and go to a night club; she lived for the sparkle and glitz of night life escapades. Frances's nocturnal habits caused her mother and sister considerable embarrassment because the neighbors would gossip.

WAR BABIES

The Second World War was on and men were shipped overseas. Ben, my father, was vague and unclear about the details of the birth in 1943 of his son Mitchell. Grandma Molly and Aunt Martha shared the responsibility of taking care of young Mitch in the small one bedroom apartment on Sterling Place. Frances's habitual preference was to go out on the town. Night life and glamour suited her better than caring for a mistake, an unwanted child. Our mother was already an alcoholic; and as so many of her generation, a chain smoker. Drinking and smoking were an integral part of Frances's life – they were glamorous! In photos, she is rarely seen without a cigarette in hand. Men were in and out of her life.

In 1942 Frances got pregnant with Ben's child, who summarily went off to war in the Pacific. At war's end he returned, married her, and they had me. Martha had divorced Nat (the horrific tale of what led to our aunt's ill-fated marriage would be revealed by her years later) and moved in downstairs with Grandma. Frances, Ben, Mitchell, and I lived upstairs in Sterling Place. Married life didn't suit my mother. She and my dad were soon divorced. Grandma Molly would say that Frances had a sexual hold on Ben; and sex was certainly not a thing of the past for her after divorcing Ben. Left holding the bag - a boy and girl, bills, and a bundle of psychological problems – our struggling mother's need for escape exponentially increased. The cracks in mental stability began to show; although in those days the effects of alcoholic intoxication were seen, at least by Molly and Martha, as mental illness - "she's acting crazy again"! Sterling Place became too cramped and nerve wracking.

Frances could hardly handle her two little ones. Grandma Molly did what she could to help with the babies yet was

 already weighted down by having to deal with our cousin Mark's violent episodes which increased as he grew older. Martha raised Mark by herself while financially supporting her mother. She helped raise Mitch and me as well; all the while keeping track of her sister's mood swings and attempting to mitigate their devastating consequences on the entire family. Home, under the collective thumb of her mother and sister, meant trouble to Frances and was too depressing. Cooking was foreign territory since she never learned from her mother how to boil an egg. Cleaning was boring; hanging up clothes unheard of.

We left Sterling Place. Frances was on the move with two small kids, and found an apartment in King's County public housing not far from Molly and Martha. Mother, dolled up and looking beautiful, would frequently go out at night, leaving us alone or asleep, after which there would be money for us to live on over the next few days. Life was painful for Frances, almost too much to bear. There were commitments into different mental institutions for months at a time because of her suicide attempts or psychotic breaks. Mental health professionals in the 1940s and 1950s believed that electric shock therapy was the best treatment for Frances's mental disorders. Aunt Martha watched helplessly as the authorities placed Mitch and me in foster care. Grandma was consumed with grief. Aggravation continued to underpin the hard life our grandmother endured. Occasionally Molly would take the two of us in for weeks at a time. I remember having to share a bed with her. At night, she would undo her bun, let down, and unbraid silver grey hair that reached below her waist. She'd brush and braid it again before going to bed. Molly mostly spoke Yiddish, especially around the grandkids when she and Martha were talking about something - our mother? - they didn't want us to understand. When sleeping at grandma's, my head would be next to her twisted and gnarled feet. They didn't smell so good but I felt safe from the world in her bed. Every Friday night she would light the Sabbath candles. My grandmother's candles sparked a lifelong flame inside of me, which often flickers and smolders but doesn't go out. I treasure the memories of staying with her in Sterling Place.

SECRET

Nightlife, men, and escape were still what our mother wanted more than taking care of little kids and assuming domestic responsibilities. Now relatively on her own, away from Sterling Place, she had it more her way. Men continued to love and leave her but one of them left behind a bundle which would continue to haunt her and the family for many of our days. In 1944, while Ben was away at war, she again got pregnant. Even Martha, who tended to know all, was kept in the dark about the father's identity. Frances didn't like to confide in her sister because Martha would often hold it against her. Grandma Molly couldn't bear yet another humiliation for the poor, struggling Goldberg family. The pregnancy would have to be hidden from the neighbors. Nobody need know about the black-sheep daughter's latest affair. The baby would be given up for adoption. Frances was removed from neighbors' prying eyes so that there would be no gossip. She was starting to show the signs of life within her; and hated being pregnant because it made her body bulge and stretch, and men weren't usually attracted to women in that state. Our mother needed to be loved and desired; pregnancy, however, was inconvenient. She could also do without, yet again, the stigma of unwed motherhood.

The immediate predicament though was how to keep her out of the neighbors' sight for as long as possible. A lawyer would help with that: Frances was put up in a Manhattan hotel until the baby was born, and at birth Linda Goldberg was delivered fresh from the oven to the glamorous couple who paid the bill. Then as if home from a holiday Frances returned to the family at Sterling Place.

A year later it was 1946 and Ben had returned from the war. Frances' youthful body was restored. Perhaps Ben felt guilty for leaving Frances in the lurch with Mitchell and decided to be there for his old girlfriend and new wife. They married later in the year and I was born one year after that. Soon, however, our mother and father were headed for divorce; and finally separated by the time I started to walk. Ben found it impossible to live with his wife. Desire was there but her mood swings, the drinking, cursing, and violent behavior proved too much for him to handle. Increasing pressure from his family clinched it; they finally divorced and he left for good. Mom would never forgive him; and at every opportunity would seek to exact her revenge, to make his life miserable. Ben as well would have a difficult time in the family courts and in keeping up with alimony payments.

Not a word was uttered about the secret baby until many years later. My father never would find out. Sworn to secrecy, Grandma Molly and Aunt Martha never revealed, until a slip from Frances, what had happened. Even Uncle Louis didn't know; besides he had a new family to care for. The Goldberg family secret would only creep out into the full light of day when dishonor went out of fashion.

ORPHANS

Mitch was seven years old. I still remember our longing yet cautious gaze, out of the orphanage into which we'd together been placed, onto the dark and scary street before us. For some reason, he'd had enough and decided that we must run away. To this day, I recall that the main topic of our discussion was figuring out how to escape without, of course, a clue as to where we might go. I was about three and didn't really understand what he was talking about. I only remember a glimmer of us wanting better lives and to not live in that place. Jimmy, the black

gardener who was fond of the young inmate, knew something was up and assured Mitch that it would all be OK if he stayed. Mitch and I would discuss this single, crystal clear memory many times as adults.

This was merely a foretaste of what the future would hold for us. We, two then three, siblings were slated over the next thirteen tumultuous years to be victims of our mother's madness. There would be several foster homes and institutions in various combinations for all three of us, together and separately. They, however, served as a respite from a violent home life with poor, tortured mother; and her almost constant moving from place to place in search of god knows what. That is until all of us, one by one, at the earliest opportunity left her.

At age one or two, my father visited me at least once in an orphanage with his mother, Grandma Rose, and his  sister Dottie whom I never got to know. They grieved because, Ben recounted years later, they couldn't take us away with them. Mother had made certain, Ben said, that he would not have the satisfaction of taking the children if she couldn't raise us; and that she'd rather let the authorities deal with us. I have vague, or no, memories of those early years except for the photos that prove I actually existed. I do, though, clearly remember Mitch and me on a New York street; and at Martha's instruction we waved to mom, who waved back to us from behind a barred window on the seventh or eighth floor of Bellevue Mental Hospital.

LIFE WITH MOTHER

Around the age of five I remember that Aunt Martha brought home a baby boy with dark curly hair, and that she placed him on mom's bed. We then lived in the Fort Green public housing project, in the Bedford Stuyvesant neighborhood of Brooklyn. We hadn't a clue as to who was his father, but we all loved our little Warren. He was

extremely cute, full of life, and our new baby brother considerably brightened our stark, bare apartment; at least for a while. I soon developed a fierce urge to protect my new baby brother from our frequently violent and abusive mother. That would prove necessary in the years to come. I had two brothers, and no inkling of a sister. We kids stuck together since, for as long as I can remember and from what I was told by my older brother and mother, we had moved at least twice a year. Because of that I was unable to make and keep friends in any school I attended. Collecting financial subsidies on the Welfare rolls was our way of life. Over the years, we lived in at least three public housing projects.

Life with mom was frightening and unpredictable. At best meals were simple and for me consisted of canned Franco-American spaghetti and Cheerios breakfast cereal - my favorites! Mitchell remembers most how she, for special occasions, would deep fry lamb chops in what seemed like a bucket of Crisco. Breakfast for our mom, almost always, was a swig of Coca-Cola and a cigarette first thing in the morning. I remember once being taken to a clinic and them telling her that I had malnutrition and that I should be eating better. I never remember pictures on the walls. There was always though a cardboard box full of clothes; they were never ironed or hung up because it was too difficult for our mom to iron anything. Every day we'd rummage through the box for something to wear.

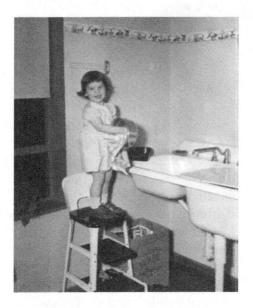

I don't recall birthday parties for any of us. There was one almost-party that almost took place in the Fort Green. I was about six and my birthday was coming up. I asked mom if I could have a party. Lo and behold she told me to invite all my friends and that there would indeed be a party. I didn't know what that meant; so, when my birthday arrived, and no one showed up because I didn't know how to invite people, she got extremely angry; that was it for birthday parties.

I had a lavender organdy dress, my favorite. When mom got angry at us she would often destroy something that we loved. I'll never forget the day she ripped my beautiful organdy dress in front of me because she was angry. The one doll I had was smashed to smithereens by mommy in a violent rage. The tantrums she'd direct at inanimate objects, though, weren't as bad as when she'd vent the frustrations of unprepared single motherhood by violently striking out at us. I was too small to remember any violent acts towards Mitchell; though I do recall the many times my long hair would be pulled by her long, hard, strong nails digging into my scalp. When I was older we lived in Kew Garden Hills, in Flushing, New York. Warren, mom, and I shared the bedroom in the one bedroom apartment. I attended Jamaica High School. At home one day she got violently angry with me. I tried to escape by running out the front door at the end of a long hallway; reaching the door I quickly turned to see where she was. That's when she hurled a big, glass coke bottle at me. I ducked just in time for the glass to splinter, crash, and splatter above my head. I'm no fan of plastic but count it a good thing that Coca-Cola made the switch to plastic bottles! I don't like drinking coke to this very day. Once, though, I defended myself when under attack. I grabbed a broom, held it in front of me and hit her on the legs. Shocked, mom stopped dead in her tracks and began to cry; then phoned Martha to hysterically complain about what a terrible daughter I was because I had attacked her with a broom. When Martha got me on the phone I began to cry and asked for her help. All she could do was to say for me to be a good daughter, go into my room, and leave your mom alone.

Our mother could barely handle stress or any situation which required care giving. Warren and I were playing outside one day when he fell on a piece of glass; it cut a huge gash in the palm of his hand. We ran into the house. I frantically asked mom to help while trying to keep my brother's wrist from profusely bleeding. She could not deal with taking her young son to a hospital and get him the stitches he needed. She just couldn't cope! So, I frantically ran to the apartment of some neighbors, and they were the ones to take both of us to an Emergency Room where Warren's hand was stitched up. When we returned home I can't remember if mother was even there. We certainly couldn't afford to have a car; even if we could it would have been a no go since mom had tried several times to get a driver's license but was always too nervous to deal with traffic or with normal driving conditions.

Frances would have passed for an alcoholic at age fifteen, and she sustained that course all through our childhood. To her credit, she never drank at home but *went out* almost every night. We never had a babysitter. She'd come home when we were asleep; occasionally with a man whose company we'd sometimes have over breakfast. Then there would be money to live on for a while. Otherwise we lived on welfare and alimony payments from my father throughout childhood. When there were food stamps and other government subsidies available we had them. Mother would wake me up, sometimes on a school night and she'd cry, tell me her problems, and want me to answer her questions. All I would think about was how tired I was, and would I be able to get up in time for school the next day?

Although, it seemed that she never kept alcohol in the house Frances frequently came home drunk. She had drinking buddies, including her longest relationship and drinking partner Charlie. He was Polish, Catholic, and she was with him for more than ten years. He would frequently stay over. They wanted to marry but his elderly mother was dead set against it because Frances was both Jewish and divorced. They planned to marry upon the death of Charlie's mother. That day never came. A telephone call one day informed our mother that her beloved Charlie had fallen to his death from a four-story building at the construction site where he worked. That watershed event triggered another stage of insanity and loneliness, the permutations of which lasted until her death decades later.

Between the verbal and physical violence, and frequent household moves Frances would *flip out* and want to end her life. Ending her life sometimes meant ending the lives of her children too. All of us had, at various stages over the years, watched and had been involuntary participants in several suicide attempts. I remember two very clearly: There was the time she blocked all the windows with towels, blew out the pilot light of the gas stove, then stuck her head into the open oven door. The smell of gas was getting stronger and stronger. I cried and asked her to please not kill us; then miraculously she snapped out of it and everything would go back to *normal*. On another occasion, she took a chair into the middle of the living room floor and stood on it, sort of like a soap box. We stared as our mother proceeded to hold a huge kitchen knife to her breast and proclaimed that it was all over; we cried and she stopped. Sometimes I would think that she might be better off dead; then I'd think about Warren and what would happen to us if she were dead. Then I'd put such thoughts out of my mind and try and concentrate on school. I also had my left thumb for comfort when things got too crazy; when I sucked it long enough a feeling of security came over me. I sucked my thumb until I was fourteen; and only after total embarrassment at a dental clinic did I force myself to stop; which was like going through what I imagine withdrawal from a heavy narcotic must be like.

GOT RELIGION?

Occasionally mother would send us to a Synagogue in Queens; she herself never went. According to Jewish tradition Mitch was supposed to have a Bar Mitzvah at age thirteen; that didn't happen because our mother got angry at the Rabbi and refused to allow her son to go through the formal procedure. Warren would later attend a school for Hebrew studies but, again, mom wouldn't follow through with a Bar Mitzvah! We really had no traditional Jewish connection, except for Grandma Molly's Friday night candles and the knowledge that we were Jewish. Occasionally Warren and I attended Synagogue by ourselves. I remember visiting the homes of some Jewish girls from school; and wondering why we didn't keep kosher or observe the Jewish Holy Days.

Mom told us about God but only that He existed, which I guess was something?! She would sometimes be angry with Him, curse her life, and blame Him and my father for giving her children to raise all by herself. I would frequently look up at the night sky, see the stars, talk to Him up there, and ask for His help. My life was like prison. All I wanted to do was escape and be somewhere else. The search for God was always there and would take me on many journeys. The one thing our mother religiously did do, during the times she was able to pull herself together, was to dress us up and bring us to the Copacabana or the Town and Country nightclubs for a night out on the town. She would glow in the limelight, and be exuberantly happy that she was able to show off her darling children to other club goers. Those times were few and far between but stuck in my memory as being fun and exciting. I remember sitting in a club, watching the floor show, and feeling lucky to have such a special evening out. Little did we suspect that our mother might have been looking for someone special, especially when we went to the Copa.

HOME, AGAIN!

Mitchell had left our unhappy home at sixteen. I was attending Junior High School in Jamaica, Queens. I was called out of class one day to be told that I had to go with representatives of the government. It was sudden, confusing and shocking. I didn't know what was going on. They would take me and Warren somewhere unknown. I was eleven and he would have been six. We were soon hustled into a Detention Home for juvenile delinquents. We were told that our mother was sick and that there was no one else who could take care of us. I didn't know what to think and wasn't even allowed to use a phone to call Aunt Martha; and I didn't know how to reach Mitchell. My little brother and I had suddenly found ourselves in a cold and forbiddingly gray institution. There were dorms for girls and boys, with about twenty-five cots to a room. The resident caregivers were massive black matrons with unkind voices; and there were all the strange children. The walls, floors, and stairways were painted a dark, shiny, institutional gray. The only time I was able to see Warren was at meals. I wasn't allowed to comfort and hold him and let him know that it would be all right. All I wanted to do was save him from the horrific experience. Writing this my heart aches with the pain and sadness of imagining what he must have gone through, at such a young age all by himself with strangers and not be able to be with his sister. How do you explain to a boy of six that your sister is close by but that she can't come and be with you? Years later after in his adult life, Warren went through the Hoffman Process and was able to process and come to an understanding of his childhood. He basically has very little memories of his young years. The Detention Home provided us with clothes, food, and schooling but there was no comfort. Other than a brief, remarkable visit and field trip with a teacher who took pity on me, we never left the place the entire month that we were there; we actually had no idea if we would ever leave. I'll never forget, though, the kindness shown to me by the teacher who went out of her way to get permission for me to participate in an international dance festival for which I had previously been rehearsing with my class. Mrs. Johnson took me into New York City, where I was able to perform in a huge auditorium. After the performance, she treated me to pizza and ice cream, and then had to take me back to the detention facility. I still remember the pain in her face as Mrs. Johnson wished me well as she dropped me off at the juvenile detention center. She was like a fairy princess who gave me hope and strength to continue at the facility and not despair. Once during the month, out of the window of my dorm, I saw a group of kids my age; and recognized that they were from my class. They were visiting the facility to show kindness to the less fortunate kids who lived there. I was so embarrassed and scared to be seen by them; I hid near my cot and wouldn't leave the dorm until they had left. Mitchell had somehow found out about our incarceration; he came to visit once but couldn't do anything because he was still a minor and wasn't able to care for us. We didn't hear from Aunt Martha; and Grandma Molly, of blessed memory, had already passed away, God rest her soul. I thought of my dad; that perhaps he could take me, but my mother had told me he was dead and that he never loved us. A month into our stay, mom suddenly appeared and took us home to our one bedroom apartment in Queens. Nothing was ever said about the month-long hiatus; and we never discussed what had happened to her or to us. She seemed okay for the moment but one never knew when she would flip out again; that, though, was the last time she would be taken from us.

Frances was a chain smoker; it wasn't unusual for her to have three or four cigarettes, in various stages of being smoked, scattered in ashtrays throughout the apartment. She wanted to get something at the store one day and took me with her. Warren was asleep and we were gone for about thirty minutes. There was smoke throughout the apartment when we returned. Our nicotine addicted mother had left one of the several ash trays in use with a live cigarette burning on the bedroom window ledge; it had fallen onto a mattress and was smoldering. We caught it in time, Warren was still sleeping.

I had a difficult time in school and was not a good student; I was always challenged to get anything higher than a C grade. Doing homework was almost impossible because mom never helped me. When I would ask for help her response was often impatience, annoyance, and yelling; telling me to go to the library and look it up. I was also envious of and disliked the pretty, rich girls in my class. Nose jobs were fashionable for many well-to-do Jewish girls and most of the girls I went to school with had had one. A nose job was pricey, so for me was out of the question and I've come to embrace my nose.

I never invited anyone to our roach infested home; and just wanted out of the nightmare I was living. I wasn't popular and didn't have any friends. I dated some guys; only one Jewish boy. I did go to parties where everyone smoked and slow danced, while listening to the Platters and to Johnny Mathis. At sixteen I went to mom and told her that I wanted to smoke like the rest of the kids. To her credit, Frances sat me down, pulled out one of her Pall

Mall unfiltered cigarettes, lit it up, and told me to take a deep breath while inhaling the smoke. I choked and choked and never smoked another cigarette after that.

One positive thing I did was teach myself how to sew. I figured that one day I would have a life of my own and could then make clothes that I wanted. I concentrated in Home Economics class and my first herringbone jumper was not bad. I remember while in sewing class, hearing over the loud speaker that someone had assassinated President Kennedy. People were crying in the streets. I felt sad but didn't understand why I felt that way. I ended up graduating from Jamaica High School but wasn't able to attend the graduation or prom because we moved to upstate New York a few months before the graduation. I never had any schoolmates over to our unkempt homes; I was embarrassed both by our furniture and lack of it; but we always moved with our trusty cardboard box of clothes.

I was in my last semester at Jamaica High School when mother declared that she was going to marry a man whom I'd get to meet only when we moved to the small town of Harriman, New York. The marriage and the move meant that I wouldn't be able to complete my senior year and graduate on time. My English teacher, Mrs. Fishman, was concerned; and invited me to stay with her family until I could finish the semester and graduate. Amazingly, mom allowed me to live with her for the last few months before graduation. Mrs. Fishman's home was beautiful and I felt like a princess. The family didn't yell and scream at each other and actually seemed happy. I wanted that and must have imagined that if I survived my life with mother, I would someday have a normal and stable life. The key was to survive.

Mother seemed happy for a while. She'd met and married Charles Rainer who adored her. He was soon to find out, however, that his new wife was abusive. Charles moved Warren, me, and mom up to Harriman. He bought a large, new mobile home in which we lived at Harriman Junction. I got a job flipping hamburgers at the junction rest stop, and decided that I should go to a community college in order to get away from my still unhappy home life. Before I left for Orange County Community College I met a young man. We stayed up all night and drank. That was the first time I was drunk and I didn't like it. He drove me back to the trailer at six in the morning. I was scared that I would get the wrath of mom when I walked into the trailer so early in the morning. To my surprise, she was sitting quietly; tears filled her eyes when she saw me stagger in. She didn't yell and wasn't mad; she just sat there seemingly heartbroken and said, "I just don't want you to turn out like me". I was shocked. Years later I'd recall what she said and try to change the course of my life.

The last time I experienced a maternal suicide attempt was at eighteen. I was preparing to leave for Community College. Warren was thirteen and had no other choice but to remain with our mother. Frances was depressed after beating up her new husband. She couldn't seem to express her frustrated emotions at that point in any other way than with the stove and pilot light routine. That was it for me; I'd had enough and I wasn't going to just stand there and watch her put the towels around all the windows and turn on the gas. I went to the medicine cabinet; and was shocked to see at least twenty different types of prescribed medications of all colors, shapes, and sizes. I gathered them up, went to the kitchen, and proclaimed, "Wait a minute, don't do it that way, here's an easy and sure way out". I threw the pills at her, they scattered all over the floor, and then I left. She cried and probably called Aunt Martha; no doubt she thought I was a horrible daughter. I wondered at the mess I'd made; and that it was very bad of me to throw her pills all over the place; and about how she would ever sort the pills out and back into the right bottles?!

Life at Orange County Community College was boring and hard. I didn't have the motivation to be a conscientious student and so I lasted only six months; and ended up working at the Homowack (Iroquois for "where the stream begins") Hotel in the Catskills. Mitch had just returned from his first trip to Europe and Morocco. He came to visit me at the hotel employee dorms where I lived. He spoke of his year and a half of travel experiences, and of *groovy* San Francisco, and his far-out friends. It all sounded so bizarre, foreign, and exotic. He had become thin and tan; and promised to help me out if I wanted to start a new life on the West Coast. Why not? This was my chance to escape and I thought that anything was better than staying in New York, struggling to make money as a cocktail waitress. It was 1965, I was eighteen, and desperately needed a change. This was the chance to get away from our mother and be my own person. I saved tips for six months and bought a one-way plane ticket to San Francisco. I told mom of my plans then left New York for greener pastures. Flying over California I saw all the vegetation and that somehow made me feel as if I was an adult; and that I could now shape my own life; and that my nightmare was finally ending. The future was here now and everything was about to radically change.

GROOVY

The Haight-Ashbury neighborhood in San Francisco was the place to be at the end of 1965. What came to be known as 'flower power' was beginning to sprout there. Mitch's top floor apartment at 555 Clayton Street was decorated with Eastern art and strange pictures that made no sense to me. The I-Ching served as his bible; and there were many extraordinary looking people in bare feet, wearing velvet clothes with long, brightly colored beads hanging from head to toe, with flowers in their hair standing, squatting, smoking, snorting, and lying on the sidewalks. 'Spare change?' was the mantra intoned by almost every other person sitting on the street as we made our way across town. The sounds of cable cars that clambered up hilly streets were so unlike Brooklyn, Queens, or Harriman. The old, wooden buildings were painted in vibrant and incredible colors; and formed an extraordinary landscape so pleasing to my eyes. After my first night at Mitch's we headed over to see his friend Diane. She was about ten years older than me and a very youthful looking woman with long, straight dirty blond hair that fell way past her shoulders. She was petite, sweet, and soft spoken with a southern drawl. Diane's smile was beautiful, and her high cheek bones accentuated her attractive face. Her apartment off Polk Street was old but not decrepit. The mixed and matched antique furniture, beaded lampshades, and cushiony pillows strewn all around, was delightful. I was welcomed in as Mitch's sister from New York with open arms and a hug.

I was soon ushered into the living room, and into another room with a scene quite bizarre to me at the time: five men were comfortably sprawled on the floor and perched upon low, legless couches. They were smoking something out of strange looking pipes and from what looked like cigarettes but didn't smell anything like mom's Pall Malls!

Hanging above the couches, and all over the walls, were enormous canvases brightly painted with wild colors of figures and shapes I could barely make out, nor exactly determine what they meant. The eyes of the long haired and bearded men seemed to have difficulty focusing on me but were friendly. I thought that the group looked unclean and grimy and I vowed never to date anyone like that. They were speaking English but I couldn't understand what they said. Moving slowly, they one by one left Diane's apartment. Mitch, Diane, and I talked for a bit, and before I knew it I became Diane's new roommate. That was it, quick and easy; the next thing I knew I was out looking for work and immediately found a job as a receptionist at Eldorado Insurance Company. I also took a training course in Keypunch Operating. Diane and I would share the apartment on Polk Street.

A few months later Diane's artist boyfriend Barry, who was to become her husband, got me stoned for the first time on marijuana. I was on my way to meet a friend and Barry said that I seemed uptight and tense. He was a nice guy and I liked his smooth, mellow ways. I really didn't know what he meant by uptight, but it didn't sound like the way to be, at least not in that environment. By then it was about two weeks since I'd arrived from New York; and decided that I should allow myself to be talked into taking just a couple of tokes on a joint. Barry played the "Girl from Ipanema" on the stereo while I sat in the rocking chair. Diane and Barry were there to gently induct me into their melodious world. I was instructed to take a slow, deep inhale. I remembered my experience with mom's Pall Mall, so was cautious about inhaling too robustly. I took a shallow puff and nothing happened so I took a somewhat deeper toke. Barry suggested I lay back, listen to the music, and just relax. I must have been anxious because as soon as I laid back everything seemed slower. I felt nice; and before I knew it I was *stoned*. Mission accomplished! They sent me out on my date. I really didn't know where I was going but somehow found my way.

I made it back in one piece and went to work the next day. I didn't want to get stoned all the time so I saved doing it just a couple of times a week; and then eventually it was as much as I liked, which was pretty often. The pictures on the walls made sense now and I saw myself transforming into a different sort of girl. My clothes seemed too tight and fitted; I wanted loose garments and I liked those beaded things. My hairstyle changed; and I began to wear my long, dark hair straight like Diane's and sometimes I would have it braided. Even though my outward appearance changed I continued to work and stay *straight* so that I could do my job. There were frequent psychedelic rock concerts at the Fillmore Auditorium and Avalon Ballroom. The strobe-lights and light shows helped when free-dancing to the music of Jefferson Airplane, The Grateful Dead, and Janis Joplin. Scott dropped into my life one day. I now had a forty something male friend who introduced me to Macrobiotics and mind-altering drugs such as LSD, mescaline, and peyote. He was a beatnik rather than a hippie. We got along. Scott was a jazz drummer and jammed in the jazz clubs then all over town in North Beach, the Fillmore, and the Haight. Scott had been part of an informal group of San Francisco jazz musicians which, in the early 1960s, would jam every Saturday at the house in which Mitch then lived with his friends Bob & Connie; they would pioneer light show technology later on in the decade, winning an Emmy for their work with T-Rex. At the time, Bob and Connie were experimenting with reel to reel tape recorders; so, musicians would make the weekly trek out to the house on Geary Street; to jam, record, and critique themselves in playback. Scott's nickname in the group was Mr. BeeBop! In only a few years the jazz scene would almost entirely disappear, as California Rock took its place. Many rock groups of the day consisted almost entirely of displaced jazz musicians. The long riffs, a signature of particularly Californian rock music reflected jazz origins.

WILT THE STILT

One night sitting and watching Scott perform at a jazz club in the Fillmore, I was approached by a waitress who said that a gentleman across the room, Mr. Wilt Chamberlain, would like to buy me a drink and have me join him at his table. I wasn't yet Scott's official girlfriend so I said, "yes". I sat with Wilt at his table and he invited me to his house on Twin Peaks 'to visit his two big, black dogs'. I knew that he actually had the dogs because they were a common sight; he'd often drive with them through the streets of San Francisco in his big, black Bentley convertible. The dogs would be seen immensely enjoying the ride, in the back seat with the top down. I was flattered that he liked me, and when Mr. Chamberlain asked for my phone number I didn't hesitate to give it to him. Looking back, I can't imagine that I was clueless about his intentions. When Scott finished his gig, he came down and asked me what had happened. I was vague, and somewhat proud that such a major celebrity would actually be interested in me. The next day Wilt called and I accepted a date with him to drive up to his house on Twin Peaks. I was excited and happy that I was going out with Wilt Chamberlain, the famous basketball player. Scott dropped by Polk Street, almost immediately after I put down the phone, to witness my gloating about the date next day.

Scott self-interestedly proceeded to enlighten me about the likely scenario which would unfold on Twin Peaks. I became gripped with alarm and imagined the worst; but how could I get in touch with Wilt to cancel since I didn't have his number? I couldn't sleep that night and was in a panic up until the time to meet him. I kept my promise and at the appointed hour timidly went downstairs to await him. He was prompt in his Bentley; but didn't open the passenger door for me so I got in myself. Anxiety gripped me as if seeing him for the first time. I noticed the size of his huge lips that would easily cover half of my face if he kissed me. His head was twice the size of mine; and although his 7' 2" body fit comfortably inside the Bentley there was little room to spare. At 5' 3" I felt as if a tiny ant against Wilt's enormous frame. His hands were bigger than my entire head; it was scary. I talked fast and, boldly but apologetically, said that I'd made a big mistake and wouldn't be able to go out with him. He didn't like that one bit. His facial expression changed from happy to see you to not at all pleased with what he was hearing. Mr. Chamberlain was angry, very angry; he started yelling and told me that I was a nobody and didn't know what I was doing. The last words I remember as my heart raced and pounded were, "Get out of my car"; which was exactly what I did, again saying sorry to have mislead you but good-bye. I ran upstairs, so relieved and thankful that Scott had saved me from being yet another of Wilt Chamberlain's ten thousand plus female conquests. Scott and I became closer after that.

MR. BEEBOP

A few months later I moved with Scott to Clement Street out in the Avenues and began a Macrobiotic life style which, mercifully, didn't last very long. Scott liked young girls and I think that I was just another pretty face to him. It didn't take me long to figure out that I needed an apartment of my own. Before moving out I noticed that my period hadn't come and discovered that I was pregnant with Scott's baby. I was nineteen and not ready to become a mom. It was the mid-1960s and abortion was illegal in the U.S., but not in Mexico. Scott offered to pay for, and arranged, the entire affair. I was frightened because I'd heard horror stories about girls dying after being butchered in Mexico. The weekend before I was to head south of the border I started bleeding and was rushed to the hospital where I had a miscarriage. Scott and I peacefully parted ways and I moved closer in to an apartment on Baker Street.

SHE'S BACK!

A couple of weeks had passed; I began to settle into my new place and the doorbell rang. Opening the door, I was flabbergasted: my thirteen-year-old brother, Warren, was standing there, suitcase in hand! Was I dreaming? Apparently not; but how had he come all by himself from New York to San Francisco with only a suitcase, and not even a telephone call to warn me? He was, of course, welcome to stay with me but how was I going to take care of a teenager still being one myself? He had to attend school and be cared for. We didn't want to inform our mother, but in the end practicality prevailed so we called to let her know that Warren had arrived safely and was staying with me. Mother told us both that she was planning to join Warren and me for a new start because she was now divorced and ready to move on. Why didn't that surprise me? What could I say? See you in a few weeks, says Frances, and I'm bringing Pixie. That wonderful female, canine creature was mother's faithful mascot, the only true buddy she'd ever really had. Pixie ended up living to about fifteen. Mom fed her well, and gave the dog attention and unconditional love which all god's creatures need but we never got.

Mitch was still living in the Haight. He would find our mother and brother a place to live close by. Mother was punctual. She landed, came to my apartment, and right away loved San Francisco. It was her kind of town - 'watch out people, here she comes!' Frances stayed with me for a couple of weeks on Baker Street; until she and her youngest son moved into the nice apartment Mitch found for them, in the by then rocking Haight-Ashbury district, directly on the Panhandle of Golden Gate Park. Warren didn't want to leave me, but he was a minor and had to go to school. I had no other choice but to let him go with mom. That living situation lasted for about a year. By then he'd had it and after a lifetime of shock and numbness he signed himself into Homewood Terrace, a Jewish boy's home to get away from her. My brother lived at the 'home' for 3 years and thought it was great. He remembered some of the other roommates that would bitch and moan about the food, but he enjoyed the regularity and thought the food was delicious; he never lived with mom again. That threw Frances into the worst drinking binge of her life. She began to have visions of Charlie coming to her; telling the love of his life to sober up and get straight. She drank even more; and more visions would haunt her. Frances was getting worse and there seemed no way out for her. She got romantically involved with Mike, a Russian ex-wrestler who did double duty as her drinking buddy. Strangers who really didn't know her loved our mother. All the stoned hippies would call her "groovy mama". Finally, she hit rock bottom and joined Alcoholics Anonymous. That was great, but she remained what is called a dry drunk. Frances's personality didn't change, she just wasn't drinking anymore. In any case, that was her road to recovery. She sponsored many young alcoholics and drug addicts with deep emotional problems; they could relate to her and her to them. Everyone at AA in San Francisco seemed to love and admire her; at least that's what she said. I sometimes attended 12 Step meetings with her. Her colleagues did show her respect, especially the older and wiser she became. The AA name Frances coined for herself was Hellen-back.

IF YOU GO TO SAN FRANCISCO
WEAR FLOWERS IN YOUR HAIR

As mom got sober, my involvement with drugs increased and I experimented with psychedelics. Diane's friend Barry introduced me to an artist friend. We fell in love and my life with Garrett began. He was a graduate of the San Francisco Art Institute and has continued to be an artist his entire life. We were both young and full of creativity. I had mastered the sewing machine and was determined to make men's clothes. I remember the first pair of wild pants I made for Garrett; the waist came almost to his armpits! He was gracious and was a good model for me. He loved outrageous clothes to match his full head of kinky hair, styled in an Afro that stood out about fifteen inches from his scalp. I made him shirts, pants, and vests; there were wild prints, and blooming pantaloons with flowering shirts to match. They looked great on him, and Garrett loved to display my creations. I became so good at sewing that I was able to sell my wares. Garrett was a skilled psychedelic poster maker, and was one of the first on the San Francisco scene in the 60s to print silk-screened posters. He needed a studio large enough for the silk screening, and well-ventilated enough for the fumes of poster paints to quickly disperse. Garrett's designs were original and abstract. We rented a studio in back of a garage on Harding Street in the Castro District. There we'd have to listen to the fledgling band Santana practice their Latin style music, while we printed posters to sell on the streets by Fisherman's Wharf. Santana was just starting out and they sounded okay.

We needed, of course, to make money to live on and pay rent; since I didn't have a real job at the time, because I was fully absorbed with the sewing of men's shirts and other items. I modeled once at the Art Institute for extra cash. Lying naked on a velvet *chaise lounge* I badly needed to fart but was terrified that anyone would hear or smell it. I held it in enduring intense stomach pains. I looked serene as if nothing were wrong; and earned one hundred dollars for the sitting - a lot of money then - but never went back.

I returned to the Art Institute with Garrett for a Halloween party. Someone came up to us, his hand stretched out with orange powder in his palm. We didn't know him, but he looked nice and invited us to have a taste. After a couple of seconds thinking about it we dipped into the orange powder and licked our fingers clean. Three days passed with no sleep, loads of sewing, and lots of printing; we then realized what we had done; but who cared at that point? We now had much more inventory to sell at Fisherman's Wharf!

Silk-screened psychedelic posters and groovy men's shirts were a good combo to sell at the Wharf. Garrett and I now had a profession; being street vendors was our gig. The problem was that selling on the streets was illegal at the time; and the City of San Francisco wanted to do away with the rapidly increasing numbers of street vendors. The authorities forbade us to sell our wares. What were we going to do? We had a lawyer friend, Michael, who used to get high with us. He liked Garrett's art work. We took the City to court; and were a precedent-setting case. Presenting our case before the Appellate Court, we were absolutely blown away when we won. Because of us people could now get legal vendors' licenses to sell their wares on the streets of San Francisco.

Garrett and I moved to the Mission District and lived on Via Linda Street. We had a small one bedroom apartment and I decorated it like Diane's place. Garrett's twin brother Kent had just come home from Vietnam and stayed with us for a while. He talked to us of exotic places where hashish was easy to get. Non-touristic exploration of the vast, diverse world outside America's borders was the happening thing to do then. The vibrant American economy of the 1960s meant that extensive travel was possible for ordinary young people who had the urge. My brother Mitch had already traveled to and from Europe and Morocco. Why were Garrett and I missing out on that kind of life? We decided to become world travelers and discover what life out there would offer us; it could only stimulate our creativity to experience new and far-away places. We didn't yet have enough money to travel; although there was enough money for drugs and rent. We began to save, an entirely new concept for us. Both of us agreed that the American political scene of the time, dominated by domestic conflict over the Vietnam War, left much to be desired. In our naïveté and budding enthusiasm for travel we thought, perhaps accurately, that there had to be better places to live and experience life than America. We'd been in at the Be-In in Golden Gate Park, had witnessed demonstrations against the war; and now were hungry to experience life in other countries. San Francisco was beginning to stifle us. Garrett wanted to broaden his horizons and stimulate his artistic talent. We decided that I would go to work full time at a real job and save enough money so that we could both transport ourselves and travel throughout Europe for an extensive amount of time. We would get to see the art of the ancient world and gain an entirely new perspective on life; and be able to smoke and purchase the best hash in the world. I went to work as a switchboard operator and Garrett made and sold lots of posters.

Frances had married George Garrett, her third and last husband; he seemed like a nice man. George donated a 1950-ish black Chevy to us, which we prepared for travel on the road east across country. Over six months we'd saved more than one thousand dollars. Before leaving we travelled to Fresno, California and visited Garrett's parents to say good-bye. Wanda, Garrett's mom and his step father, Tom, editor of the Fresno Bee was supportive of our decision to travel. They were concerned, though, for our safety and didn't really want their son to leave but couldn't hold onto him if they tried. They did the next best thing with encouragement, and threw us a going away party. Tom and Wanda were sweet but of the old school. It was obvious that we were living together unmarried. They didn't allow us to sleep in the same room; but made us a tasty going away cake, with camels and desert scenes decorating the top. We said good-bye not knowing when we would return to America, although we knew that a great adventure was before us.

ON THE ROAD

Garrett's brother Kent was part of our immediate adventure and played a big part in our lives over the next six years. It was 1968 when, in the Chevy, we headed east on Route 66 across America. With three of us driving it took one week to cross through the many States to reach New York. We had an easy time of it except upon entering Little Rock, Arkansas. The police spotted us – well, they at least spotted Garrett's Afro. I was driving while Garrett and Kent were urging me to go faster. The speed limit in town was thirty miles an hour, the exact speed I was careful to drive. The police car never pulled us over; but you could taste the negative vibes as he tailgated us out of town. Little Rock wasn't ready for any hippies in their town; but we did get a police escort through Little Rock.

We were pulled over once on Route 66 by a highway patrol man. He said we looked like wild Indians. Little did he know that in the back-seat Kent and Garrett had stashed at least twenty joints of marijuana in a plastic bag. There was some truth in the cop's statement because Garrett and Kent were direct descendants of Uncas, a great chief of the Mohegan Tribe. Sitting in the car I looked out the side window and only saw the trouser legs (the Rashomon effect?) of the patrol man who was at least six feet tall. He eventually let us continue on our way, and we got out of there in a hurry.

We reached New York City, our destination. As soon as we arrived, we visited Aunt Martha. Uncle Louie was also there and gave us a camera for our travels. They wished us well and Aunt Martha packed for us a huge bag of sandwiches, donuts, and other pastries for our transatlantic crossing, scheduled to leave in a few hours. Kent took the car and drove it back to the west coast. I'll never forget the excruciating Icelandic Airlines torture flight. What a nauseating ride: fourteen hours of intense buzzing from the engines, while the whole plane shook without stopping. The smell of fuel filled the crowded cabin. We stopped all too briefly in Greenland to refuel and then onto Belgium. After disembarking with our backpacks, bell bottom pants, granny shoes, beads, my long hair, and Garrett's fuzzy Afro, we heard the first words of greeting from the locals - shouts of, "Hippies"! Maybe the Europeans hadn't seen anything like us before; perhaps they had?! We spent our first night in an ancient French style hotel. It was so incredible to actually be in another country where a language other than English was spoken. It seemed so foreign, because it was. Everything smelled differently: the sheets, towels, and the air. The food too was so different. That was the beginning of a four-year adventure which would take Garrett and me around the world. We had no plans or expectations, and few clues about what we would encounter.

EUROPA

After our first night's sleep in Belgium we woke up to our first continental breakfast. Even the jam tasted better to us. The architecture of each building we passed would seem to pop out at us; it all was ancient and bursting with centuries of tradition.

Garrett and I talked about what to do now that we had finally arrived. There were no plans and between us we still had about one thousand dollars. We would spend it wisely, and thereafter stay in hostels instead of hotels. We had one backpack each and were free to do whatever we wanted. There were as yet no destinations in mind; we'd just go with the proverbial flow. We bought a map of Europe, sat and thought, and recalled where Mitchell had once recommended to go for relaxation and inspiration: the small island of Ibiza off the coast of Barcelona, where he had spent an idyllic summer in 1964.

Now we had a destination, and accordingly planned our route. The first stop by train would be Milan, Italy. The main train station of the city was in the center of town; and we somehow found our way to the student building of a university. Perhaps someone inside would help us figure out where to stay, and tell us how to get to our next stop on the way to Ibiza? All we knew was that Ibiza was located in the Balearic Islands, and that you got there from Barcelona. Up until then our travel strategy was to go, stop, eat, and to get stoned along the way. We entered the building and saw that many of the students were getting ready for their vacation from school. Both Garrett and I were outgoing and friendly; and the students were attracted to us by the way we looked and dressed. They had heard about Hippies from San Francisco and here were two live ones. Paolo and Antonio, two guys who spoke some English approached us. We talked, and used our hands to communicate; and Garrett could draw anything to get his point across. Before we knew it, they took us under their collective wings; and put us up in their apartment for two weeks. We toured some Northern Italian country-side, visiting Lake Como, Lecco and

Lugano. We met their parents and got high together. It was oh so cool to our new Italian friends that we shared with them the drugs (which they totally enjoyed) that we'd brought with us from San Francisco. Even though we couldn't fully communicate with each other we got our points across. They also wanted to experience the freedom they saw in our lives. We took pictures, and shared with them stories of living in America, and about our plans to travel on to Ibiza. They drove us to a hitch-hiking place on the highway that would lead us in the direction of Spain. We cried, hugged, got out, and started to hitch through Europe.

A huge semi-trailer truck stopped, picked us up, and drove us to Genoa, Italy our next destination. We stayed in youth hostels along the way. While waiting in Genoa for the boat that would bring us to Barcelona, we purchased various items, especially one, a stiletto knife that would come in handy one day in the not too distant future. The hour arrived and it was time to board the big steamship to the Catalan capital. I hadn't before traveled by boat and it didn't at all suit me. I was sea-sick and stayed on deck the entire time; the better to throw up overboard my dears.

We at last reached Barcelona and quickly made our way to purchase tickets to Ibiza. Since it was going to be another overnight journey on a boat, this time we got a sleep cabin. I wasn't thrilled about yet another boat ride, but we couldn't afford the short but expensive plane ride to the island. Money was going fast. We could only anxiously think of getting to Ibiza and finding something there for us to work at. I reluctantly boarded the ship that held a few hundred passengers. Garrett and I stayed up late; waking early to behold a sight which would capture our hearts.

THE MED

The Mediterranean Sea: there's nothing like it in the world and Ibiza is in the middle of it. After the eight-hour boat ride from Barcelona we woke up to a beautiful morning; a clear, blue, sky was reflected in the crystal blue water of the Mediterranean that surrounds the Balearic Islands. We slowly, gradually, reverentially approached the island of Ibiza; our senses were overwhelmed by the myriad white-washed stucco houses that, with charm and grace, terrace above each other while fitfully hugging the craggy mountain cliffs that line the shore of Ibiza Town, the island's city center. There was the harbor, where dozens upon dozens of small boats and yachts dock. A sharper outline of the beautiful, green island emerged as we got closer. The hills and trees that seemed so far away a few minutes ago were now almost within swimming distance, as if I could swim that far. I had never before seen anything so beautiful as that first sight of the old city's harbor backed by hills that seemed so close I could touch them. I still recall standing on deck staring at the sight, and thinking how fortunate I was to have come all the way from the tenements and housing projects of Brooklyn to this remarkably beautiful place. Garrett was also much impressed but perhaps not as much as me. He and his twin brother Kent were born and raised on the island of Oahu in Hawaii. They had been fully exposed to exotic island living; for me it was an entirely new experience.

Approaching the harbor, it became clear that the native Ibizinquos were wearing mostly black; especially the elderly women who wore lots of it. They were covered almost entirely in black. Since it was a hot and humid day, I felt sorry for them in their heat absorbing dark clothes. We gathered our few possessions, made our way down the plank to dry land, and entered at last the destination we had sought and travelled far to reach.

IBIZA

We had to find a place to sleep and leave our backpacks. From the port, we approached the old city, zigzagging through narrow alleys and cobblestone streets; then through an old stone arch that would lead us deep into the ancient city of Ibiza. Making our way past old, piled on top of each other white-washed stone houses, we were directed to the *Pension Oliver*, a charming hostel run by a Swiss couple; Mitch had stayed there when he first arrived in Ibiza four years before. After renting a room

for a week, checking out the local hash market, and getting our island land legs, we rapidly adjusted to our new life. We bought bikes so that we could independently roam around the small island.

After a week, making numerous contacts with young foreign visitors, we realized that it would be wise (and we'd save money) to rent a house outside the center of town. We found an old two room stone house to rent a couple of miles from Ibiza town. For fifteen dollars, monthly we had secured a charming, although primitive, little home. There wasn't any electricity but we stocked up on kerosene lamps and candles. The kitchen had a bucket and we cooked on wood. There was no running water; but the main house where the owner lived was not far and we were able to get water there. The outhouse was close by.

Garrett would draw and paint the surrounding, ancient olive groves and terraced stoned walls that seemed to meander all over the island. I soon found work at a newly opened leather shop in the old city; because of my sewing skills I was immediately hired. The owners, a French Canadian and his American wife, taught me to make from scratch men's leather pants; a talent which would come in handy later on in our travels. I worked at the shop making all kinds of leather clothes: pants, jackets, vests, and skirts. I diligently worked and we all got along very well. A couple of Italian brothers from America invested in, and expanded, the leather shop. The wares now included sandals, belts, and bags. It was a thriving business. Garrett found work with a local artist and continued to do silk screen production.

We met and hosted many young travelers from all around the world in our little two room stone *finca*. They'd regale us with stories of their travels and where to score good hash. We knew the prices that people were paying for hashish in the States; and it was obviously profitable to buy hash and sell it in the US. We supplemented our income by sending hash to Kent in San Francisco. He

sold it at good prices and then sent us the money. We had creative ways of hiding the merchandise and miraculously never got caught.

We were also visited by my brother Mitch; on his way to the American University of Beirut in Lebanon on a junior year abroad program from the University of California at Berkeley. We needed a bigger place to live more comfortably and moved into an old *Ibizinquo* stone house equipped with a water well. There was a long rope and bucket with which to draw the water from outside the back door. The outhouse was a little closer, and the kitchen was out the back. We now had a real wood burning fireplace instead of a makeshift one to cook our meals. The rent was only twenty dollars monthly, and the house had two bedrooms, a living room, and lots of land. We still needed lanterns because there was no electricity.

MOROCCO

Mitch told us stories of his adventures in Tangier, Morocco. It was a good place to go in order to get a renewed visa and the hash was supposedly good. Kent was on his way to stay with us in Ibiza. He arrived with a blonde Norwegian girlfriend. They stayed in our new house while Garrett and I made our way by boat off the island: destination Tangier! After a couple of days traveling by bus and thumb via Malaga and Cartagena we reached the Rock of Gibraltar. There were many sights to see along the way. Our main purpose though was to exit Spain before our six-month visas expired. After reaching the port of Algeciras we hopped a ferry to cross the narrow Strait of Gibraltar to Tangier. We couldn't avoid noticing, upon leaving customs, that many people were searched as they entered Spain from Morocco.

The boat was full but the ride relatively short. On board, we met a young Moroccan man who spoke good English. Ahmed was immediately drawn to Garrett. He was sweet and very warm; inviting us to meet his family in *Assilah*, just south of Tangier on the Atlantic. We took his name and number and would contact him after we arrived. Landing in Tangier was awesome. Walking up into the city proper from the port, we were met by a dazzling array of extraordinary looking people, and smells of spices and Moroccan cooking. Women were covered from head to toe; only eyes showed, framed by their flowing *djellabas*. The colors and smells of the Muslim country were vivid and exotic. One boy tried to sell me beads from Mecca. I learnt the art of bargaining in Morocco, as I soon became adept at successfully haggling for dramatically lower prices. I dove in like a duck into water, and was able to purchase beautiful treasures at reasonable prices. We took up our new friend's offer and visited him in *Assilah*. The bus there was filled with locals, their chickens and goats, and cornucopial baskets of food everywhere. Women seemed to hold everything on their heads; and all but the kitchen sink would fit snugly under their robes, making them bulge from the wares they sought to conceal from passersby.

After about a half hour out from Tangier, and according to the instructions Ahmed gave us over the phone, we got off at an unpaved roadside stop. When we reached our destination, our friend was there to meet us. Garrett couldn't wait to try some local hash. That was his dream. He and I were both invited into a local smoking parlor; where all sat in something like a circle. I was the only woman there. The men's heads were covered with various turban-like headgear, and were smoking from water pipes. I stuck close to Garrett in fear of being swept away, off my feet by one of the strange but interesting looking men. Our new friend could see that I was uncomfortable sitting amongst them, so Ahmed invited us to his home a ten-minute walk down a dirt trail past weathered white stucco dwellings. People walked barefoot around the animal feces everywhere. I tried to avoid stepping in shit but it was almost useless after a while. I felt like a snob when attempting to avoid the animal droppings and I wasn't even walking barefoot. Then I walked without caring where I stepped. We finally reached Ahmed's family home; even though they all looked the same to me. There were stucco benches outside the doors into the houses. A hole in the ground was near each home; I later discovered they were the source of drinking water for families in the area. Ahmed introduced us to his family. They welcomed us into their home with open arms and true hospitality. Ahmed was the only one who spoke English, and we certainly didn't know Moroccan Arabic or Berber.

The family were Berbers, indigenous inhabitants of North Africa. They lived differently from the city dwellers in Tangier. We were invited to stay as long as we wanted. Garrett was thrilled because now he was one of the guys; he'd learn to smoke like a local, and enjoyed every minute he could with his new-found pals. The women served us sweet mint tea with tons of sugar, and food I can't begin to describe that tasted strange but was very tasty. After a few days, "it" hit me - a dreadful case of the runs with severe gastric pains. I couldn't move and every time I did, "it" would end up running down my legs and then I would have to wash. I was embarrassed and in lots of pain. Everything I ate or drank immediately passed right through; "it" went on for a few days. I thought I would die. Garrett went into town with Ahmed and brought back medicine. Meanwhile his mother invited friends by to visit the sick American woman. They tried to help me recover and no doubt entertain themselves when instructing me how to belly dance. They had a battery-operated cassette player that played Arabic music, while they each got up and coaxed me to get up and dance. I appreciated their efforts but couldn't move. They were very sweet but I couldn't communicate anything, except the pain on my face which loudly proclaimed that if I moved I'd have to run to the outhouse! The body lingo spoke louder than any words. The women wanted to help, but I was in excruciating pain and tried to be pleasant but it didn't work.

Garrett returned with antibiotics and they worked; getting me on my feet so that I could walk without the constant ache of abdominal pain. Afterward, amoebic dysentery would haunt me for years before getting it out of my system. Watching the children play by the open water hole, and seeing all the dirt and dust going down into the water didn't help either when I'd drink the hot mint tea. There was no such thing then as bottled water, and we couldn't be so rude as to ask the family to boil the water for us. The women continued to be kind to me. Whenever I was finally able to walk outside, and would begin to sit down on the stucco bench by the door outside the house, someone would come over and immediately place under me the skin of a goat or sheep to protect me. I was treated like a queen. The women would dress me up in their best *caftans* and Garrett would wear a Moroccan *gandoura*, with the stripes and colors of the family's clan. They wanted us to stay longer but we had to return to our life in Ibiza; so, we said our farewells and promised to return on another visit.

We made our way back to Ibiza and would return to Morocco at least one more time to renew the Spanish visa. We didn't go away empty handed though. Garrett made sure that he had a stash of hash to last him. He loved hashish, it inspired him to create impressionistic paintings and drawings. Even though I indulged, I was a lightweight compared to him. Remarkably, we weren't caught on the way back going through the security check at Algeciras. In Ibiza Garrett had enough for himself with some to sell; with the profits, he bought a motorcycle. We had real wheels now to travel the island. I had my bike and never liked the motorcycle; it scared me, and I never had confidence that I would be safe on it with Garrett. One rain-stormy night we went out for a ride; I kept saying as he rode down the wet narrow road, that I wanted to go back home. A lightning bolt struck directly in front of the bike; after that Garrett thought that it probably was a good idea to turn around and return to our simple but dry home.

Kent lived with us for months. There was tension between him and his brother; mostly, though, the tension came from me: I'd had enough of listening to both of them, one on either side of me, talking into one ear and out the other saying the same thing over and over. It made me crazy. I complained to Garrett, to no avail, that we needed our privacy and our own lives; but he was loyal to his twin and, no matter what, Kent could do no wrong.

Six months went by and we left for Morocco a second time. We briefly visited our Berber family and made some other contacts along the way; including Tom, an old friend of Garrett's from San Francisco. We were to help him purchase a large quantity of hashish in Tangier, and were to receive a commission. A local who seemed honest enough, led us to someone who sold Tom about ten kilos of the stuff. We had a Volkswagen van; and someone Tom knew was driving back into the city. As we approached a crosswalk, a blind man stepped into the street and our van came to a screeching halt, as we had almost hit the blind man. A Moroccan policeman saw what happened, pulled us over, and told us to follow him. We stopped at the back of a police station and were told to empty the contents of the van onto the sidewalk. Incredibly, the hash-filled duffel bag was never looked at, and we were told to go. Unloading the van at our destination, we sat with relief in contemplation of the eventful day. I opened the bag and couldn't believe my eyes; it was full of henna instead of hashish. The color, a pea green, is similar to hash but the smell is distinctly different. That I knew because I'd used henna to color my hair.

We traveled more through Morocco this time: to Fez, Marrakesh, and back up to Tangier; all the while collecting different types and grades of Moroccan hashish. Garrett and I were sitting in a local cafe, drinking hot mint tea, and watching the crowds go by. A nicely dressed Moroccan approached Garrett, and they immediately struck up a conversation about Garrett's favorite subject. The friendly Moroccan man, Mostapha, asked Garrett the magic question, "Do you want to learn how to make your own hash"? That was an offer which my traveling companion could not refuse. Mostapha said we should both come by his apartment at eleven that night. We were staying at a cheap local hotel and I was tired, but we both ventured out into the dark streets of Tangier to locate Mostapha's apartment. Making our way through narrow, dark, and stinking alleys we finally found the building. In the small apartment, I sat in the salon while Garrett followed Mostapha into his kitchen to learn how to heat and press the fresh female marijuana resin into hashish. Meanwhile, I overheard our host tell Garrett that he wanted to sleep with me! My ears perked up when I heard that; I couldn't believe what I was hearing. Heart pounding, I almost panicked when I heard what Garrett said in response: "I don't think she wants to, but you can ask her". Mostapha came into the salon and point blank said that he wanted to sleep with me. I said, "absolutely not" and that "I want to leave"! Garrett then pulled out his stiletto from Italy, began to leisurely clean his nails with the needle-sharp tip of his knife, and told the over-friendly Moroccan that he didn't want any trouble and that we needed to leave. Mostapha quickly opened the door and let us out; but another man was standing just outside the door; and we made a run for it, through the late-night streets of Tangier desperately trying to find our way back to the hotel. We must have been quite a sight; a hippily-perverse Kodak moment to be sure.

Back on Ibiza, we felt safe and content. I continued to make leather clothes and bought a treadle sewing machine that didn't require electricity to operate. Garrett completed a large, abstract painting he sold for a few hundred dollars. Our creativity was expanding and improving. We met a wonderful Dutch couple from Amsterdam, who invited us to visit if we ever made it up to northern Europe.

A BAD TRIP

After a year and a half of living on lovely Ibiza something happened at a wedding of two hippie Anglo residents which turned both Garrett and me off. Their marriage ceremony was celebrated on the small island of Formentera near Ibiza. The journey to the island was an all-day event. Many of the locals living on the small Balearic island knew the couple and came to the wedding in order to wish them well. We joined others crossing in a small motorboat to get there. In about thirty minutes we arrived. The bride and groom took their vows. The party was in full swing with loads of food and fruit punch. The guests, both young and old, drank and ate their fill; and before we knew it the last boat was leaving back to Ibiza. We made our way back but noticed that something definitely wasn't right. Garrett and I had had both good and bad experiences while taking LSD together; this trip was turning into a bad one. At first, we didn't realize that a drug was causing what we were experiencing. There were hallucinations of all sorts. When we finally made it back home, which seemed like hours, I remember looking at the counter tops and screaming, because it looked as if thousands of bugs were crawling over them. Garrett convinced me that nothing of the sort was happening; but he was experiencing other hallucinations. Hours later we recovered from the LSD-laced punch; but felt so bad for the local people and others, unsuspecting victims of an irresponsible group of stoners; some of the new wave of visitors to the island who had the attitude that *everyone must get stoned.*

It was time to leave; a year and a half had passed. We didn't have much to show for ourselves, except for my sewing machine, and Garrett's art supplies and his motorcycle. We had saved some money from working and what Kent had dutifully sent us from the States. Garrett came home one day and said that he'd bought a van for seventy-five dollars from a traveler he'd met at the post office. It was a British diesel cold-storage sausage truck; insulated and big enough to live in. The van was bigger, wider, and taller than a VW van. What a shock; what were we going to do with a big van on the small island? Garrett had it all figured out: we would drive our home on wheels to Amsterdam, live in the van and work, save money, and then go overland to India; which is exactly what we did.

The nice Dutch couple we'd met on Ibiza had already invited us to Amsterdam. The husband produced a local children's animated daytime TV show called *Fablestizgrant;* a highly popular show in the Nederland. Garrett would work there as a set designer. Before leaving Ibiza, we'd fixed up the van with the essentials we would need for the journey. Garrett built a hinged loft in the main section of the van, over the driver/passenger

cabin that served as our bed; with a mattress and about twelve inches of head space when lying down. By day, half the platform folded up, and was secured by a hook to the interior roof, so that there would be both more standing room inside and usable daytime storage. The main cabin held Garrett's art supplies; a mini-kitchen consisting of a one burner pump kerosene camping stove, pots and pans, dishes, and utensils were my domain. I couldn't live without my treadle sewing machine, so we put it at the back of the cabin. The two back doors when opened swung out, so I was able to sew while enjoying the scenery. I'd purchased lots of Spanish leather to take north; and there was a trunk with clothes (shades of our clothing box?); and pillows on the floor for sitting and reading. The driver's section of the van was wide and comfy; the two captain style seats in the front cabin were separated by the huge diesel engine that did double duty as a table for drinks and food. The two side doors next to the seats slid open. The driver's side was on the right because the van was from England.

We had purchased, and held, our tickets to ride! The fully loaded van was on the ferry and we crossed the Mediterranean one more time. From Barcelona, we headed north to Amsterdam. It was summer; the climate was nice and the journey, which took about a week, was relatively peaceful. We met other van travelers along the way.

We immediately looked up Niek and Roos, our Dutch friends in Amsterdam and camped out on a picturesque canal. We'd back up to the edge of a canal, and when we opened out the van's back doors there was complete privacy from the street. Boats would pass; and the graceful swans were lovely as they glided past our door. We obtained working visas so finding work wasn't difficult: Garrett worked on the TV set, and I got hired at IBM as a Key Punch Operator. I worked in the Administration Office; and although I couldn't speak Dutch, got along well with everyone - especially my boss who wanted me to stay and become an instructor with the company.

Garrett and I toured different parts of Holland on our days off, and we managed to save money by keeping to the vision of driving to India as our main focus. I made one side trip to London to visit Mitchell. He was living upstairs from, and worked at, the As You Like It cafe` on Monmouth Street; near Covent Garden that then still functioned as

London's central market, and the great city's beating heart. A train and a ferry took me across the English Channel. How refreshing it was being in a country where I could understand what was being said! I'd made a point of learning the basics of the language in every country that I found myself in, so that I could at least buy food, change money, and greet the locals. I stayed with Mitch

for a few days and got the royal treatment. In England, I learned to drink my tea with milk. We took a day trip to Chelsea where we had our picture taken under a tree in the back, (by a photographer friend of Mitch's who lived there, off the King's Road) where Henry VIII had Thomas More arrested for not granting him a divorce.

Back in Amsterdam the weather was changing. The increasing cold made it unpleasant to live inside a cold-storage sausage van! If it got cold in the van it would stay cold because of the insulation. Our Dutch friends wanted to help us out so they moved into another apartment for three months, and gave us their own apartment in the middle of the Red-Light District. It was interesting to meet the ladies of the night at the local laundromat; where they looked radically different in daylight, from when they seductively sat in their red-lighted picture window sitting rooms that faced onto the canal. There were many ethnic restaurants in the neighborhood. One night at an Indonesian place, I noticed that someone who had entered was wearing a familiar looking vest. I could hardly contain myself; eventually I approached the stranger and asked from where he'd gotten the vest. He had recently purchased it from a leather shop in Ibiza. I gleefully told him that I had made his vest; we both were surprised and delighted and I started to realize just how small a world we lived in.

MEAT ME TONIGHT!

One day we were getting high with some local artists who lived near Amsterdam's Central Train station. I remember hearing the trains go by, listening to stories they told about what happened during the Second World War when the trains would be loaded with Jews for transport to the labor and death camps. It was eerie hearing the trains rumble by; chills went down into my bones and I felt uncomfortable being there.

Our main purpose, though, was to discuss a project with one of the artists, known for making posters of shocking pictures with catchy sayings. Someone asked if I could sew a coat out of meat; "sure, why not"? I replied. Before I knew it I was hovering over at least fifty pounds of fresh, red, beef steak filets. On butcher paper, they were placed on the floor of the apartment; some sort of powder was constantly sprinkled on them to keep their freshness and bright red color. I had to work fast. The end result was a full-length coat sewn in patches of steaks. The long sleeves had fat on the cuffs and the coat's hem was trimmed in fat to both complement the cuffs and aesthetically bind together the whole coat. A beautiful and sophisticated naked blonde model alluringly positioned a filet mignon across her crotch. She wore the coat partially open to reveal her bare breasts. The poster's caption read, "Meat Me Tonight"! First glancing at the poster the coat seemed made of ordinary patchwork; but upon careful examination you would clearly see the detail of each steak, and the fat dripping around the edges. That episode turned me vegetarian. Meat disgusted me and I wouldn't touch it for years to come.

Winter set in and Amsterdam got extremely cold. If we left northern Europe and headed for Turkey we would be able to avoid the worst of a harsh winter. I purchased an oversized full length brown bear fur coat (without the bear's meat attached!) in the Amsterdam flea market for the equivalent of five dollars. Since there would not be sufficient heat to comfortably live in the van while traveling in the winter, I would not only wear it but we'd use it at night as a blanket and it kept us warm.

We eventually did find a charming, small, black, wood-burning stove about two feet high that would do the job. Because we needed ventilation to let the smoke escape and not asphyxiate us inside the van, we cut a round hole in the insulted side metal wall of the main cabin behind the driver's seat, and ran a stove pipe out through the hole that extended up and over the van. It worked; and we looked like the Beverly Hillbillies of Europe. We had to make sure though that we didn't let the stove get too hot because then the pipe would turn red hot and could easily burn up our house on wheels. Burning wood a bit at a time did the trick of keeping us warm during the winter months without burning our mobile home down.

After eight months of working and building friendships with our Dutch friends, we said our good-byes. The associates at IBM didn't want to let me go but I was determined to go to India. I don't recall why it exerted such a strong pull on me; perhaps it was the lure of exotic India, adventure, or just the experience of having the total freedom to do it. Others had driven the route we were to take. Kent crossed the Atlantic and drove on ahead of us. He would meet us in Delhi. It was biting cold when we left.

TURKEY

We backtracked through Europe, down to Yugoslavia. Compared to Amsterdam it was nice weather but we had to cross a huge mountain range. Ascending one of the mountains, it seemed forever before we reached the peak. We needed snow chains on the tires because of ice at the summit. Cars and trucks were sliding everywhere; we could barely keep the van from going off the road. Everything was white and iced over. I was petrified and thought we would go off the mountain; but we made it down to warmer climes. Traveling into Greece we'd only spend a couple of days passing through. Our next stop would be Turkey.

The drive through Turkey in winter is not an enjoyable memory. Traveling through the northern part of the country was not what we had expected or planned for. We'd foolishly imagined date palms, desert, and camels. We got ice, blizzards, and frozen icicles hanging from the mouths of enormous horses that hauled sleighs; resembling something Omar Sharif would drive in Dr. Zhivago. The horses' cruel masters wore bundles of fur that covered their near frozen bodies. Even with our new wood stove, we froze while driving in daylight. Want to experience Siberia without going there? - northern Turkey will do just fine! It snowed so hard and thick at one point that the windshield wipers couldn't work fast enough to push away the heavy snow that completely obscured our view of the road. I'd never seen snowflakes that big. We soon learned that diesel fuel freezes; and since our van used diesel, whenever we parked for long the fuel would freeze. How were we to drive without a flow of fuel to the carburetor? We had to both defrost the diesel and use a spray can of ether on the engine located inside the front cab. How to defrost a tank of diesel fuel: Garrett would light mini fires under the gas tank outside and wait just long enough so that some of the fuel would be defrosted; I would start the engine on the inside, but not wait too long because the tank could explode. The routine would happen every time there was freezing weather, which was how it was all that extraordinarily cold winter.

Using a public toilet in Turkey then could be a nauseating experience. We'd become accustomed to squatting with feet straddling both sides of a hole-in-the-ground toilet. The holes were usually flush with the ground, and the feces would go down far enough to just flush or leave. We were used to it and besides didn't have any choice. When you gotta go, you gotta go; and no matter what you had to do to do it you would do.

We stopped one day near a small shop in the middle of a small town. We both desperately needed to use the facilities, and we somehow conveyed our desperation to the elderly men who, trying to keep warm, sat around drinking Turkish coffee. There were usually no problems in conveying our desperate needs. Garrett let me to go first, which was uncharacteristically sweet of him. In the tiny room that reeked of shit I could hardly believe the sight before me: a pile of frozen, multi-colored fecal matter that formed a cone-shaped solid, emerging about twenty inches above the floor of the hole! I had to hold my breath and stop from vomiting, while simultaneously trying to relax so that I could deposit my little contribution to the pile; all the while trying to keep my balance and not fall over near or onto the Mount Everest of crap. The face I made to Garrett upon exiting the room must have said it all. He came out with the same look on his face, and we laughed about the experience for years to come.

Driving on northern Turkey's mountainous roads I spied, out of the corner of my eye, a dark, furry blur darting across the floor of the van. I freaked out! I had driven through all kinds of situations, had braved the cold. I was someone who had fearlessly smuggled across international borders and was a certified global traveler; but could not accept that a mouse was sharing my living quarters. I screamed as if someone was about to kill me. Garrett was driving, clueless as to what was going on. We were winding through a mountainous region so he couldn't stop to see what the matter was in any case. I jumped on the passenger seat, kept screaming, and got hold of the broom we kept to sweep out dirt from the van, and had this way armed myself in protection from the furry little fiend. Garrett finally pulled over. I didn't come down off the seat until he captured the mouse and expelled it.

Garrett discovered a potent Turkish drink called Raki (Arak) that turned smoky white when added to water. He loved drinking it but it didn't like him. Maybe because of his Indian blood he couldn't hold his liquor, but that didn't stop him. One night we managed to get some relief from the cold by staying in a local hotel; it seemed like a nice place and was cheap enough. We took hot showers, slept in a warm room, and would begin our journey across Turkey the next day. It was late, Garrett had had a good dose of Raki; I was exhausted and we climbed into twin beds and fell fast asleep. I woke up with a strange feeling. The room was dark. I tried to focus my eyes on the door that was being opened. A dark figure covered in a blanket entered. I froze with fear and couldn't move a bone in my body. I somehow got the nerve to pretend I was waking up and moaned and tossed from one side to the other. The figure was headed for our clothes draped over a chair, that contained our passports and money, but decided to quickly leave the room. As soon as he left, the lights in the room came on and off, seemingly by themselves; or was someone from the outside making it happen? I had no idea what was taking place. Garrett, my protector, was so plastered he didn't wake up during the entire episode!

Even though his bed was not that far from mine I couldn't get close enough to shake him; but I got my voice working and began calling his name; first, at just above a whisper; then higher pitched and frantic as the lights continued to go on and off. I began to yell his name, loud as I could, but no response as yet from Garrett. My body was at the point of sheer exhaustion, and I was angry because he wouldn't respond to my pleas for help. I began to shake him, with still no response. After more shaking Garrett roused himself, wondering what on earth was I doing to him in the middle of the night? Then he got sick, quickly got up, and made a bee-line to the toilet and threw up his Raki. At first, he didn't believe my tale, but I was convincing and frantic and he finally understood what had happened. We locked the door, and pushed a chair under it to prevent the would-be thief from coming back into the room. Lying back down, I couldn't sleep but Garrett had no difficulty returning to deep slumber. Early the next morning we spoke with the owner; who confirmed that one of his employees had been caught stealing from the guests, and that he would call the police to arrest him. We didn't believe that would happen. A fire was lighted under the van and we were on the road.

The Iranian border was only a few kilometers away; but it was late at night so we stopped at a local restaurant and ate. It was still freezing cold. Our fuel was low, but we heard that once in Iran, on the other side of the border, we could refuel. We didn't want to stay too long at the restaurant because the fuel would freeze; then we'd have to wait until morning before we could start a fire to defrost the fuel. Garrett couldn't resist one last drink of Raki, before entering Iran where alcohol would be hard to get. What the hell? He got drunk; even after our horrendous experience of the night before! Little Miss Perfect me wouldn't touch the stuff; and I watched and dreaded what would happen when he got behind the wheel. Even though we had shared the driving all along, Garrett insisted that he drive to the border.

It was dark, cold, and snow was everywhere on either side of the narrow two lane road leading to the Iranian border. Road traffic was not English style, so oncoming vehicles were on the left. I had a good picture of how close things were, since my head was relatively clear. In the distance, I saw approaching two big, bright lights. We were used to them, as many Big Mac trucks traveled the roads; and we were familiar with the light signals each made when passing in the night. Some drivers would turn off their lights, so that another vehicle on a dangerous curve could pass without having the blinding lights of an oncoming vehicle blind him. The Big Mac truck approached on the narrow road. I strongly suggested to my inebriated chauffeur that he stop and pull over, because there wasn't enough room on the road for both vehicles. No way! He just kept rolling along as if nothing could possibly go wrong. My suggestions became stronger, higher pitched, and resulted in a demand, but still no budging from Garrett. (He was going to prove his point no matter what, and I was going to learn that Garrett couldn't perform well under the influence of alcohol). Now, I was screaming, pull over, pull over! I was right; we didn't have enough room; and at the very last second Garrett realized it, and swerved to the right. We ended up in a snow bank! Thank God for the snow bank and that it was winter; otherwise we would have gone over the cliff. Now we were stuck in a snow bank, with our van tilted at about a seventy-five-degree angle. There was no way we could get out alone. Feeling totally disheartened and discouraged by our circumstance, Garrett decided to do nothing, but complain that no one was going to stop and help us.

Our fuel was low. If we turned off the engine it would freeze; and being stuck in the snow bank didn't give us the option of lighting a fire under the gas tank. If we ran out of fuel someone would have to go and get some. Although I kept insisting he do something, I thought better of it and decided that *I* better do something before we both freeze to death. I had on my big, brown, bear fur coat. I climbed up, rolled the sliding cabin door open, jumped down from the van onto the road, and waited for traffic heading towards the border. Along came a nice couple who stopped and promised to send someone with a truck back to help us. About fifteen minutes later another Big Mac truck appeared. The driver saw our predicament, got out his chains, hooked them up to the front bumper of our van, and backed his truck up while I was inside hanging on for dear life. The van tilted to the right and we heard a loud, expensive grinding noise; but we were finally on the road again. We profusely thanked the driver. I was happy to leave Raki country behind for good. We managed to make it to the Iranian border before running out of fuel; with enough remaining to keep the engine running until the sun came up. We passed into Iran with little difficulty but our troubles had only just begun.

IRAN

That first day in Iran I will always remember. We had just crossed the Turkish/Iranian border in the dead of winter. Everything was frozen; we needed gas and our map pointed the way through a little town. Then we heard it: a grating, metal sound coming from under the van. We limped into a small border town where we asked for a mechanic; we barely made it there before the van wouldn't go any further; but it was a hole in the wall. There were no sidewalks in the town, only dirt roads. Nobody spoke English. Since we had British license plates everyone thought we'd come from England. People warmed themselves from fifty-five gallon drums set ablaze. What looked like a junk yard of car parts were pushed into the tiny store front of our mechanic to be. It

 was 1970 and Iran was beginning to go through changes. We hadn't a clue as to the political situation; all we cared about was getting to India. The Shah of Iran was still in power, and even though he was allied to the U.S.,

Americans were unwelcome in this part of the world. We resembled a stoned, clueless Mr. and Mrs. Magoo, nearsightedly traveling the world together. We had a nonchalant outlook and basically liked everyone; but were almost totally unaware of what in the world was going on. There was no English radio or newspapers to get information from; so we had travelled without understanding our surroundings or circumstances. When we came across other Anglo travelers, we'd ask about updates in the world; but we essentially missed about four years' worth of world events during our travels. I still don't know if that is good or bad?!

The van had miraculously stopped directly in front of the little hovel of a mechanic's shop; that's what local people indicated through sign language and some interpretation. Garrett asked for his help; and a few hours later the mechanic emerged from under our van with a round metal wheel the size of a dinner plate, called a Grand Pinion Differential. Half of its metal teeth were ground down; and some teeth were totally missing. He explained to us that it was impossible to fix, and that we needed a new part and, of course, there wasn't anything like that available in the small town, or in any town close by. We'd have to travel to Teheran in order to get a new part. Garrett and I had to make an important decision. Our options were: 1) Abandon the van and all our possessions; 2) Both of us go to Teheran and leave the van unattended for at least one week, since Teheran was about five hundred miles away; 3) One of us go to Teheran, while the other stays with the van to protect it from thieves. Option three seemed our only viable choice. A woman traveling alone in Iran was not advisable. Garrett had to take the differential to Teheran and try and find a replacement, in order for us to continue our journey to India.

The first night alone in the van was terrifying. The only weapon I possessed that I thought could cause some damage should anyone break in to try and hurt me or to steal something was a baseball bat. The sun went down and Garrett was off to Teheran by bus. Noises outside the van began; there was banging. People tried to determine who was inside, and if they could break in or pilfer van parts from the outside. Access to the engine was from inside the cab; so, the only thing they could get would be the tires. I had wood burning in the stove to keep warm and the outside pipe was too hot for anyone to touch.

When I heard, anyone approach and bang on the van, I would yell at the top of my lungs and bang the bat on the van's metal walls. That made it clear that whoever was inside was angry; and if anyone tried to get in they would have to deal with a banshee witch - I do banshee witch well! But I didn't sleep well that first night. I consoled myself by curling up under the covers, and under the almost magical protection of my bear coat. It was winter, it was cold, and I was alone in an obscure part of the world.

The next morning, I awoke and started a warming fire. I ventured outside to survey hostile territory in the light of day. Everyone seemed fixated on me: I know that I stood out like a sore thumb; a western woman alone in a small Persian town. I tried to conceal my fear but was anxious, and not at all certain that Garrett would return. Next to the hole-in-the-wall-garage was a hole-in-the-wall-bank. A nice looking middle aged man, wearing a suit, came up to me from inside the bank. He spoke English well and I was happy to talk with him, but I still harbored unpleasant memories of Tangier, and was guarded. He said that if my husband had gone to Teheran he wouldn't be able to make it back for at least a week. The nice fellow had already discussed the issue of our van with the mechanic and knew our situation. He suggested that I go with him to his house, and that his mother and wife would be very happy to let me stay with them until Garrett returned. He insisted that it wasn't safe for me to stay in the van alone, and that he would take personal responsibility for making certain that no one would destroy or steal the van. It was a tough decision, since I didn't know this man from a-hole-in-the-wall town. Even though he seemed sincere and honest could I really trust him? I decided to take a chance and trust the words of the stranger. To my surprise, amazement, and relief he took me directly to his home; where his wife, Farrin and mother, Habibeh, who only spoke Farsi, welcomed me with open arms. I was there one week with the family. I didn't know Farsi, but made myself understood using sign language and drawings. We even made crafts together; and I got to experience delicious homemade Persian cooking. The week passed all too slowly and the family could tell that I was concerned about Garrett and about what would happen to us if we couldn't get the van fixed.

Garrett returned with the differential in hand. After searching vigorously throughout the city, he couldn't find the new part we needed, but had managed to find a welder who welded more teeth into place to make the existing differential useable. This would be both a blessing and a curse until we reached Nepal. The mechanic quickly installed the rehabilitated differential. We thanked the banker and his family and drove off into the still wintry weather of Iran.

AFGHANISTAN

After a few days, we entered Afghanistan. Approaching Kabul, the differential broke again; it made the familiar grinding noise that had before brought us to a halt. We soon learned that it's not a good idea to weld metal teeth onto a differential, because most of the stress of the vehicle is put onto the differential, and it takes the most tension. The search for another part began; and we ran into the same problem of trying to find an English car part in the middle of a foreign country; this one-half Russian and half Afghan. The part didn't exist there so we chose to go again with welding, instead of abandoning our movable home and its relative security.

We had again entered a country we knew nothing about. We were globe trotters with no sense of direction or context. We spent a month in Afghanistan. Garrett found a source of hashish, and there were sights to see like dog fights; the dogs were big as ponies. There were mosques to visit up in the hills. We attended what looked like a polo match; there was a dead goat tied onto a horse, that dragged it over a huge, muddy field. That's *Buzkashi*, Afghanistan's national sport; a sight out of the Arabian nights, with all the costumes, head coverings, and wild colors of the horsemen who clubbed the dead animal to smithereens.

We spent time with Muslim families who invited us into their homes. Everyone liked Garrett; he was very friendly and spoke the language of hashish which the men understood. I was, of course, always sent to where the women were. Garrett was never allowed to follow me and I was not allowed to accompany him. He found drugs and I found women behind their veils. Afghan women found me a curiosity to say the least. I was a female Westerner, who had traveled from America all over Europe; and now lived in a van heading to India. They couldn't figure me out; but I was a compliant source of entertainment for them, and that was just fine; it was such a privilege to be invited into the homes of the Afghan women. Most of those I had the privilege of meeting were marked with the scars of small pox all over their faces. No one but their female friends and close relatives, and of course their husbands, were allowed to see their faces. Some had

 deeper scars than others, but almost all the women I saw had smallpox scars to prove they had not escaped the disease.

The Afghan women reminded me of the Moroccan Berber women of *Assilah*. They too enjoyed performing for me, dancing to their music. The Afghan women liked to examine my clothes and show me the outfits they wore under their *burqas* (the long dark robes that cover Afghan women from head to toe; with only a small mesh veil that allows them to breathe and see out of). No stranger would know who was under the veil. Once crossing the border, I looked over at a man accompanied by his covered wife. He was holding her passport along with his own to present to the authorities. As I peeked over, to see what her picture looked like, I saw a photograph of a covered woman in a *burqa*. Only the husband could identify her because no other man was permitted to look at her face. I felt sorry for these women but they didn't seem to feel sorry for themselves. Of course, I wasn't able to have an intelligent conversation, or for that matter any conversation with them; but with the women I met there seemed to be a universal language which women can speak to one another without verbalizing. The eyes say so much, as do facial expressions and hand gestures; body language speaks volumes. There was a camaraderie amongst us, even though we came from different worlds. We somehow understood each other and had respect for one another. Even though I didn't wear a *burqa* and nobody forced me to, I tried to respect the customs of the countries, such as Afghanistan, which I visited. I would at least cover my arms and legs but, of course, I was still regarded as a Western woman. That I was a Jewish woman never ever came up. I wonder if that would have made a difference? I was, in any case, blissfully ignorant of problems between Muslims and Jews.

Life in Afghanistan was not a piece of cake, but brownies are a different story: the most memorable time of our month in Afghanistan was when Garrett, who had scored some "good stuff", wanted me to bake hash brownies. I had a propane gas top oven we had picked up on our journey; so, I baked him a pan of brownies. I ate one. Garrett didn't stop eating until they were all gone. Three days later I was finally able to lift my head off the pillow and feel alive again. The hash brownies didn't seem to affect Garrett in any detrimental way. A month later, we got the van fixed by welding on the metal teeth again. We had some sandals especially made to hide Afghan hashish in the soles, and headed for the *Khyber* Pass.

Down around, down around, and switch back after switch back that didn't seem to end is my recollection of the *Khyber* Pass. Tan, brown, and gray; the Pass was almost completely desert terrain; with more rocky, mountainous landscape than I had ever seen. We were getting closer to our destination and just one more country to pass through - after Pakistan we would enter India.

For some reason, I had a romantic vision of what India would be like. I got a taste of what it would be like as we finally reached Pakistan. Hot humid weather was as big a challenge as freezing in our insulated home on wheels. We stayed in Pakistan for only one night before making our way to the border.

INDIA

At the Indian border a policeman entered our van. I thought he was looking for drugs; and even though we hid them well, we'd heard horror stories from travelers along our way - in Turkey, Iran, and Afghanistan; many young druggies had traveled these roads before us and had been caught out. Garrett and I were two American hippies, ignorantly and naively smuggling hashish across perilous and dangerous terrain; in countries with governments which could care less about putting young drug traffickers away for life. Young travelers we'd met along the drug route had also scoured the Asian hashish trails for the best, freshest, and purest they could find and many were behind bars. We met numerous young women, trying to obtain the release of boyfriends out of Turkish and Iranian prisons for drug possession. One young woman was in tears as she told us how she had finally mustered five thousand dollars to bribe jail authorities; only for them to turn her away saying she needed another five thousand to have her boyfriend released. There would still be no guarantee that they would honor their word. Years later I would see the movie Midnight Express; it frightened me to think that I could have been in one of those Turkish jails. A thought of divine protection may have been one reason why I was never caught. Would I have committed suicide rather than endure something so horrible?

Even knowing the reality about what might be our fate we did it anyway, defying the odds that we would be caught. Maybe it was our turn to be arrested when the Indian policeman entered the van. He seemed nervous and secretive, and handed me a paper bag; he said hide it somewhere in the van. Getting off as quickly as he got on he would meet us on the Indian side of the border. I searched for a place to hide the rather heavy bag, and decided to peek inside and saw only a few bottles of wine. Hardly a word was uttered and we obeyed the authorities; which is what one did in the countries we journeyed through. I joined Garrett up front and we entered India. Our policeman stamped our passports and waved us through. We drove a little way down the road and he came up behind us, entered the van again, thanked us and took his package. Off he went with his bottles of wine. Now we were smuggling for the authorities.

Any previous romantic visions of India were soon dashed to pieces as we drove to New Delhi, an eye-opening experience of a lifetime. Mangy mutts in skin and bones strolled village roads. Snooty holy cows took their time wending their way through the streets of cities, as people made a sincere effort to respect their presence. One word to describe India, though, is "people"! They are everywhere you would go. Out in the middle of nowhere there would be within two minutes, hundreds of people asking the same questions in proper English: Where are you from? What are you doing here?

Not only had we to continue using the ubiquitous hole in the ground toilet, but there wasn't any toilet paper; we soon came to realize that the water spigots inside the toilets were to wash our bottoms after we dropped our offerings. Now we knew why one must always wash with the left hand, because Indians eat food with their right hands and the twain must never meet.

Along the dusty dirt roads, we saw big birds lining both sides of the roads. They were gigantic and we soon realized they were vultures - ugly creatures waiting to profit from death. The smell of death is everywhere in India. The Hindus burn their dead in the streets on top of funeral pyres. The sickening smell of burning flesh permeates the air. It's a smell that, in my darkest moments, I imagine Poles must have been aware of as the bodies of Jews were burnt to ashes in nearby crematoria.

Finally, the weather was hot as we reached India. Our van didn't have air conditioning so we had to endure extreme heat inside the cold-insulated cabin. We were extremely thirsty driving along a dusty road one day. A big hand-written sign in English caught my eye for, "Ice Cold Beer"! You never saw someone who doesn't like to drink beer, guzzle down an ice-cold beer so fast. We would in time learn that it's better to drink hot tea during hot weather since one's inner body temperature becomes hotter than the atmospheric temperature and you actually feel cooler than if you consume cold drinks.

Driving along Indian roads we saw rock piles lining the roads. They began as huge piles of large boulders. Men and women would break boulders down to smaller size rocks. Then another huge pile of the smaller size rocks was further broken down by other people into pebble sizes; then even smaller piles were broken down into gravel, and then again into almost a powder; a common sight along the roads. If I didn't see it with my own eyes I wouldn't believe it was possible to have three men working on one shovel. One man pushed a shovel into the dirt; another man pulled a rope attached to the bottom part of the shovel to help pull the load out of the dirt; and then a third man would help the first man to dump the dirt onto a pile.

Although every bit of garbage was used for something, there was the sense that everything was dirty. In New Delhi, we met up with Kent. We spent days exchanging stories of our experiences and how all of us had managed to meet in India's capital city. Together we stayed in New Delhi for about a week. Garrett and Kent decided that the place to go for the best hash in India was to Kashmir up north. Kent had heard rumors that one could go into a field, rub off the fresh resin of the female marijuana plant, and gather your very own hashish by yourself. It was not exactly true but Garrett almost always believed his brother.

We stayed briefly in a youth hostel for the hot showers, and we discovered what it means to be a subject of the Indian caste system. Several of my IBM colleagues in Amsterdam had told me that Indians were better off living under a caste system. I didn't understand what they meant, but felt uncomfortable to think that a human being would be considered inferior for being born into a certain family. In the courtyard of the youth hostel a man was cleaning the nearby toilets. I had to use one and after I came out noticed that he had dropped something. I automatically reached down to pick it up and hand it to him. He was very thin and dark and wore just a simple loin cloth. He gave me an anxious look when our eyes met as I handed him what he had dropped. He didn't like it, and I couldn't understand why he was so frightened. He was *Dalit*, an "Untouchable", the lowest of the low in the caste system. It's forbidden, it was later explained, for a non-*Dalit*, especially a white *mimsab* (superior Western woman) to help him. I continued to defy the caste system as often as I was able. I didn't care what other people thought of my actions. Perhaps I thought of myself as being born into an American caste system, which I had broken out of. The big difference is that I had had the freedom and choice to break out.

There were many beggars in India, always holding out their hands to ask for *Baksheesh* (alms). Many were deformed by birth defects, diseases, and accidents. We were told that some poor families actually maimed their children in order to gain sympathy and bring in more money begging. When I think of the India I experienced decades ago, melancholy tinges my memories of the sights and sounds of that distant land.

We mapped out a route to Srinagar, Kashmir; and the three of us together made our way through the mountains of northern India. The countryside was extremely beautiful and looked peaceful, until we stopped for the night. Within five minutes at most the van would be surrounded by hundreds of inquisitive people asking the same questions: Where do you come from? What are you doing here? Do you have a mission?

Approaching Kashmir, we entered a two-mile-long tunnel, with a narrow one-way lane; with no lights inside the tunnel! It was unnerving as we neared the tunnel's end. When I was a child in New York, we would be driven through the Lincoln Tunnel, or another, under water. I was terrified that the tunnel would collapse, and that the water would rush in and drown me. I would hide in the back seat of the car and pray we would get through safely. I felt like doing that but knew better than to go and hide my head. We finally saw the light at the end of the tunnel.

Coming out of the darkness into the light, the scene on top of the mountain seemed out of a fairy tale. Everything was green and hilly. The mountains were lined with terraced rice paddies descending all the way down to the valley of Srinagar. The air was clean and there was beauty all around. The drive down, of course, was relatively quick compared to the ride up. We entered the town of Srinagar to sounds of the old, familiar grinding noise. Unknowingly we limped into the Srinagar Police Station facility; it looked like a nice place to park and nobody chased us out. We lived there for six months until we were ready to leave. A war between Pakistan and India was about to break out.

KASHMIR

The three of us made the best of a bad situation while living in Srinagar. The beauty of the lakes, Moghul gardens, numerous other sights, and the lush landscape of Kashmir, stimulated our creativity; however, we were stranded in our paradise! For six months, we spent most of our time trying to get our van back on the road. Mitch was still living in England, and I had his address on Monmouth Street near Covent Garden. I wrote to him with (almost) all the details about the van, and the part (the differential) we needed to get fixed. We found a local mechanic who told us that the differential was beyond welding and that we needed a new one. Our only hope was for Mitch to find and mail us the English part for our English van. We anxiously waited for his reply; which took a couple of months because of the inadequate mail system. My big brother promised us to do his best searching for the part and, when found, would mail it to us. We waited, trusted, and believed it would come. Meanwhile, we occupied ourselves with eating, touring, making friends, and brushing with the law.

Once the van was securely parked, and we had removed the differential, it would be extremely difficult to move to another spot. There we were, truly and inescapably, stranded in Srinagar! The police enclosure also served as a place where local men could take public showers. We would open the back doors, though, and Garrett would draw. I cooked, sewed, and watched people bathe themselves from the spigot near the van. We took trips on the river and spent time playing tourist when we visited some of the famous houseboats in Srinagar Lake. There was a beautiful Mogul garden, the Shalimar Gardens. I remember how exquisite and immaculately maintained they were, so beautiful that I wanted to savor the memory. I decided to embroider the scene: a path led down from the hill, through a vivid combination of flowers, to the small lake; where a tiny Mogul bridge connected the two banks of the Shalimar gardens. The finished piece of embroidery took me months to complete, and was made into a dark green velvet purse I would use. Years later, I wanted to frame it; but somehow the purse got lost in moving around.

Once we took a trip into the mountains; we stayed overnight in a cabin and went fresh water trout fishing the next day. We met some country women who braided my hair into what seemed like a thousand braids: first they put, what looked and smelled like, lard on my head; then it took them at least two hours to form the braids all over my scalp. The pattern they made was beautiful. Washing my hair braided so intricately, though, gave me an itchy scalp. Eventually, all I could think about was that I needed to take out the braids and thoroughly wash my head. Garrett helped me after I panicked when unsuccessfully trying to unbraid my own hair. It took four hours to get the job done! After that it took several washings to completely remove the lard and get my hair back to normal.

Two months after we'd arrived in Kashmir, Kent decided to return to America. We made sure he was well stocked with supplies, so that when he got back to the States and sold his wares he could send us some money. Garrett continued to make friends with the locals. Kashmiris are both Muslims and Hindus; and we heard that there was a lot of conflict brewing; and that it was getting dangerous to live there. So far nothing of that sort had affected us, but we were about to get a foretaste of what was to come.

A Western woman walking through the streets in India was risky. Even though I would walk with the twins, there were men who made it their mission to bump into me, and somehow manage to grab a part of my body, and then just walk away. Once, with both Garrett and Kent walking on either side of me; a man advanced, and before I could protect myself, his hand had grabbed my crotch! I was in shock. I yelled and screamed, but he went on his way; and the twins, my protectors, didn't do a thing to stop him. Another incident happened one day while Garrett and I walked to a local barber shop for a warm water bucket bath. By now I was fed up with the local men's amorousness and, on guard, protected myself as much as possible. Garrett was a bit in front because of the crowded street. Suddenly, as if out of nowhere, a male hand grabs my breast. I looked up and saw a tall young man. He let go and went on his way as if nothing was wrong. That was all I could stand. I'd had enough and began to yell and shout, and make quite a scene. After my tantrum, I went to take a bucket bath; finished, we left the barber shop. A Kashmiri policeman came up and asked me about the man who had accosted me in the street a short while ago. I didn't really understand what he was asking me. Then he told Garrett and me that we needed to go with him to the police station. We got into the policeman's horse drawn buggy and after several streets stopped at an unmarked building, then went up some flights of stairs. I never did see a sign that said Police Station. We were told to sit and wait.

They brought out the young man who had accosted me in the street; badly beaten, his hands and feet were shackled. I almost cried because I thought he didn't deserve such severe punishment for what he had done. The police demanded I sign a written statement accusing the man of a crime. I refused and they said I must do it. No, I can't do it! Then they got extremely upset when it became clear that I was not going to give them what they wanted, so they ordered us to leave. I never did find out what became of the young man. But I decided from then on that I would carry a large staff with me when I walked the streets. I never got accosted when I carried that staff.

AMARANATH

There was a yearly trek to the top of *Shri Amaranath Ji Yatra,* a 15,000 foot mountain in the Himalayas. Reputedly an incredible experience, and since we had a lot of time on our hands, we decided to trek the mountain. We started our trek at the base of the mountain range, in the foothills of the Himalayas, in the summer of 1971. The tradition and legend are that in order to see the miraculous ice formation at the top of the mountain you had to go during a particular time of the year when the moon was full, usually during July through August. Then, as the moon waxed and waned an ice stalagmite formed, by the lunar cycle, into a *lingam*, the phallus of the Hindu god *Shiva*!

Little did we realize there would be hundreds of pilgrims, *yatras*, seeking a glimpse of the divine genital on (of) ice. Along with a few foreigners and many locals were *sadhus,* religious Hindu men who roamed the country with only a staff and a pot, and usually attired in just a loin cloth. Their hair was usually long with dread-locks the *sadhus* never brushed; it would knot up, and god only knows what would grow inside the plaits?! *Sadhus* usually smoked lots of hashish; and because their faces were mostly painted with a white chalk like substance, it was hard to tell if they were stoned or not. My Mohegan liked them a lot. It took three days on the way up the mountain to reach the summit. Many people hired donkeys to carry their bags. We hiked with our backpacks the whole way and slept under the stars. The last night up we slept in a covered shed that protected us from the evening cold. Most of the s*adhus* had almost nothing on as they traveled barefoot up to Amaranth. Every now and then a completely naked *sadhu* would pass by; I got used to them and just about everything else in India. The day came for the last part of the journey, to reach the cave and see the ice formations. I can't remember what Garrett and I fought about, but he didn't go the distance with me. I finished the last couple of miles without him; I certainly wasn't going to miss the climax after three days of schlepping up a 15,000-foot mountain! I left Garrett to sit and pout and continued the journey alone. There was a glacier I had to cross; after the glacier, I saw a huge cave in the distance, my destination. The opening of the cave was about sixty to seventy feet wide and extended twenty to thirty feet deep into the mountain. The roof of the cave was about fifteen feet high. I couldn't believe my eyes; the legend didn't lie. I saw the huge lingam shaped icicle in the back of the cave. To make sure I wasn't imagining it, or dreaming, I took off my shoes and barefoot, stood on the lingam's base; I felt the ice and knew it was real! Did anyone shout at me to get off? Maybe; maybe not! I believe that I was not showing disrespect by standing on the huge, holy phallus. I turned around, took a couple of photos, and noticed a small group of naked *sadhus* smoking their pipes. Why not? I said to myself, and joined the little circle of naked men and tried the best I could to communicate with them. One of them had a tattoo on his arm. I assumed he'd left a secular life to pursue the life of a holy man. They were very kind, got me stoned, and served me hot *chai* (tea with spices and milk), and sent me merrily on my way, back over the glacier. I got back not too late, and related all that I'd experienced to Garrett who was just about over his pouting. The next morning, we headed down the mountain. Along the way we spied beautiful, little, delicate flowers growing all over the mountain fields. They were Edelweiss, flowers that grow only in very high altitudes. We didn't want to ravage the landscape so decided to pick only fifteen of them. Later, we set them in pendants that Garrett designed, so that both sides of the Edelweiss could be seen; enclosed in glass sealed with silver. We sold some and gave some as gifts to friends.

Back at the campsite we were happy to be back in Srinagar. We began to hear stories about the Pakistani war about to break out, and got nervous watching military vehicles use camouflage netting as cover.

One day Garrett hadn't returned from his daily outing of painting and drawing. I worried, and thought that something bad might have happened to him. After spending the entire night alone in the van, he arrived the next morning looking disheveled from spending the night in jail! He'd had to convince the authorities he wasn't a spy, merely an artist trying to capture the beauty of Srinagar on paper.

We finally got a notice at the Post Office that a package had arrived from England. Could it be that our differential had finally arrived? We were so excited, and could scarcely believe that it had actually been six months from the time we had broken down until the part had, indeed, arrived. We took it to our mechanic friend; with whom, by now, we were friends of the family. The van got towed to his garage; and, with high expectations, we waited for the day we could leave and head east to Nepal.

Mother of all bummers: the part Mitch sent was the wrong part. I cried a lot that day. He sent the right part but for a petrol engine and not a diesel engine. In any case, years later I learned that there was no identification of the van's type of fuel in my letter; and the differential we received was the only one available after extensive searching! Our Hindu mechanic was also concerned for our safety in Kashmir at the time. He wanted to see us leave and decided he could make it work if he jerry-rigged the differential with a cotter pin to hold it in place. How long would that hold? He couldn't guarantee how long it would, but he showed Garrett what to do if – when! - it came out of place:

The procedure was to get under the van, pull out something, and replace the cotter pin. That would take about an hour, then we could continue driving. We had confidence in our mechanic and excitedly prepared to leave town in a few days.

We stocked up on food and other supplies, said our good-byes and left. We drove up and up, and back through our long, narrow tunnel to the other side; headed down again towards Delhi but with a slightly different route along the way. One day out from Srinagar we broke down but Garrett knew what to do. He got out and did exactly what our mechanic showed him and we were on the road again. It worked! After five episodes of fitting the cotter pin back in place, we made it to Delhi.

DHARMSALA

We stopped along the way at *Dharmsala*, the home and headquarters of the Dalai Lama, in exile from his – and the thousands who went with him in 1959 – homeland, Tibet. Monks in orange and deep red robes turned prayer wheels round and round. Their gentle spirit made us want to be where they lived. We bought some art, including a little water color from one of the Dalai Lama's artists. I would later give the painting to George Harrison in Hawaii.

Leaving *Dharmsala*, Nepal was our destination. On the way to New Delhi there was more stopping and fixing of the cotter pin. It was a seemingly never ending chore, but at least we could go for a while and stay on the road. The question of the moment was what route to take to get to Nepal? Fully stocked with supplies we headed to the ancient city of Benares (*Varanasi*).

BENARES

Ancient buildings lined the banks of the sacred River *Ganges*, an awesome sight. Many thousands of Hindus from all castes, the women wearing colorful *saris*, carried trays of flowers as daily offerings in homage and worship to the altars of their gods. The dedication of the people was predictable and consistent; they seemed never to tire when it came to their offerings.

Parking the van, we began to explore the ancient city. We walked timeless, meandering streets; avoiding traffic, we made our way down to the *Ganges*. Following the crowds eventually led us to the river's banks. Countless people were bathing, surrounded by strange floating items that looked like dead, bloated animals. Taking a ride on the *Ganges* we, indeed, saw dead animals as well as other weird objects floating on the water. The man who took us out in his dinghy scooped up the water with a ladle and drank. He offered some to us but we politely refused. I almost threw up. From out on the water we looked back at the shore and could see the ancient city's buildings from another angle. Our captain pointed out that when the *Ganges* rises so does the water level along the coast, and we saw where the water left its mark on the buildings. I still don't know how the people living in the houses cope, if at certain times of the year they are flooded, but they do. We were happy to leave the small dinghy for dry land and thirstily bought some bottled water to drink and for the road.

Next was *Agra*, where we visited the *Taj Mahal*, one of the seven wonders of the world. It truly is a wonder; we spent time inside and out exploring. Tour guides told differing stories of how it was built in honor of an emperor's wife. The millions of tiny tiles used in the Palace's construction make the acoustics incredible. Instruments were being played in part of the building. Years later after seeing a TV special about Princess Di at the *Taj Mahal,* I remembered my time there. I was thankful to have been able to see the magnificent structure; a masterpiece of architecture built in the seventeenth century, it took seventeen years to complete, and twenty thousand workers to build.

The roads were terrible, and the potholes atrocious, but we passed through the rest of India without incident. The monsoons had just finished. We didn't have too many problems with the van and we almost felt that holy India had healed our sausage truck.

Nepal beckoned and there was another big mountain pass to cross before we would reach *Kathmandu.* It was very narrow and dangerous; and were told that major accidents happened all the time on the mountainous road; and that many people were killed by either landslides or oncoming traffic.

We braved the road figuring that we had been through a lot worse and by now were experienced drivers. We shared the driving in all our travels overseas. After the arduous journey, we made it to Nepal with a two-week visa, which we knew would not be enough. We'd been told, though, that it was easy to bribe the authorities into issuing one month extensions. *Kathmandu* was exotic; and we were to discover that its wildlife had as much entertainment to offer as its city life.

NEPAL

Just outside Kathmandu, on a mountain encircled by a road, we found a parking spot for the van and made *Shwyambunath* mountain our home for the next three months. The sacred mountain was also home to hundreds of Tibetans who had flocked there after China's invasion of Tibet in the late 1950s. Tibetan temples were everywhere and the Tibetans had a similar lifestyle to the local Nepalese. When we first arrived, it seemed as if all the houses had bars on the windows and we couldn't imagine why.

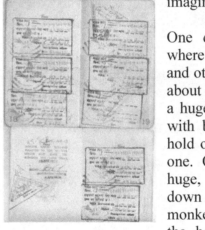

One day at the local store, where we'd go to buy produce and other items, a small boy of about three stood near me with a huge guava. He held onto it with both hands too small to hold onto the guava with only one. Out of a nearby tree a huge, male baboon jumped down between us. The intrepid monkey grabbed the fruit from the boy's little brown hands and, with his treasure, fled up the tree as fast as he'd come down. In shock from the hairy baboon's attack, the boy started to scream; at first, his face slowly contorted in order to produce sobs, which then issued forth in the torrent of screams which brought his relatives out, from inside the store to investigate the commotion. People told the boy's relatives what had just happened. I too was in shock at having been so close to the baboon. This was a daily occurrence which Garrett and I would have to learn how to deal with.

BABOONS AND BANANAS

We set up house as usual and began to explore the neighborhood surrounding our new location. The spot we had chosen, Shwyambunath mountain, was a busy thoroughfare of mostly foot traffic, but no one seemed to mind foreigners living in a van, so we stayed. It took about an hour to walk around Shwyambunath. Every day we would sit and watch the locals walk by with heavy loads on their backs; in baskets supported by a hemp strap that ran from the bottom of the basket, up and onto the carrier's forehead. That way they could carry a large load if they bent their backs forward as they walked. We noticed that many of the women who carried food in their baskets would be periodically attacked by the baboons and their food stolen. The victims would yell and scream at the monkeys and then go on their way.

Living on the mountain was much better for us than living right in Kathmandu; it was cleaner on Shwyambunath. There were huge statues in the temples of both the Nepalese and Tibetan gods; all in vivid colors, everywhere you went. Occasionally we'd venture into town where some of the sights were shocking. Kids, of no more than eight, would carry heads of freshly decapitated water buffaloes down the street just after they had been slaughtered, blood dripping everywhere. The youngsters carried the heads as normally as I would carry a bundle of laundry on my shoulders. Although a separate country, Nepal seemed as if it were part of India. Hindus cremated their dead in the streets on funeral pyres. The sickening smell of burning flesh would permeate the air.

People would relieve themselves in the streets and pigs would gobble it up.

Early mornings on the mountain we would awaken to the sound of monkeys jumping out of the trees, onto the roof of the van, and off again. We tried our best to befriend our hairy neighbors. Once Garrett was sitting on the low rock retaining wall that lined the road all along the mountain. He took out a bag of peanuts and starting eating them. Baboons smelled the nuts and soon arrived in droves to see how many they could steal. A curious and brave female sat next to Garrett on the wall, and watched intensely as he opened peanut shells and placed a nut on the wall for her to pick up and eat. The nut fell between them as Garrett fiddled around; both of them grabbed for the unshelled nut at the same time. I watched with curiosity as both the baboon and Garrett stared into each other's eyes to a standoff. When the female bared her sharp teeth, it was game over, an easy contest, and Garrett let go of his end of the peanut.

I would cook inside the van on the pump burner from Ibiza; and would sit at the back with the doors flung open to enjoy the cool breeze. Once I'd bought a *towla* (about one pound) of tomatoes to use for dinner, they were on the kitchen counter in a bowl. While sitting on a pillow with my back to the open doors, a hairy hand swiftly darted past me and snatched the entire lot of tomatoes off of the counter. Another time Garrett went to the store for some beans for dinner. He came home furious, because he'd been ambushed by the baboons; and they broke the bag of beans, scattering them everywhere. The last straw though was the banana episode.

By now Garrett and I had learned to hide everything from prying eyes and swift hands. At the market one day Garrett bought a nice hand of bananas (a whole stalk contains many hands, and this hand had fifteen to twenty bananas attached). He placed them as usual on the counter with the back doors opened. Without realizing that we were being watched, he turned around for a split second. Lo and behold, a huge male baboon with a multi-hued red butt had swiftly entered the van and stolen the hand of bananas. Garrett was fed up with all the thieving; and this was the banana that broke the monkey's back. The short, stocky baboon lobbed leisurely up the mountain and Garrett took off after him. The monkey soon realized he was being chased by a wild man with an Afro, wearing wildly colored clothes. He began to run faster clutching the bananas; his treasure firmly gripped in both hands. I stood at the bottom of the hill beside the van and couldn't believe my eyes. Garrett caught up with the baboon almost at the top of the mountain about one hundred and fifty feet away. As he gained on the short, rotund thief Garrett reached over, grabbed back the hand of bananas, and headed triumphantly down the mountain. The baboon let out a shriek, as if to say what *chutzpa* of that human to steal my bananas. That alerted all the other baboons, both males and females. They converged and ran after Garrett. He ran faster and faster downhill. Every actor in the piece speeded up, as if in a Keystone Cops silent movie. I stood awestruck and watched this hilarious scene develop. At the same time, I was scared for Garrett because I feared what the encroaching stampede might do when they caught up to him.

A daily danger facing the monkeys were the Nepalese soldiers; they would take pot shots at them as target practice. It was common, cruel and sad to watch; although a couple of Anglo hippies from San Francisco weren't about to tell the Nepalese soldiers what not to do. I thought of the soldiers and their rifles, and picked up a long stick lying on the ground near the van. I aimed it directly at the monkeys hoping that they would see, and it worked! Garrett came speeding down the hill with the clan of monkeys right on his tail; but the monkey mob stopped in their tracks when I shouted to Garrett, and they saw what they thought was a rifle in my hands. We really enjoyed eating those bananas and got lots of mileage from the banana story for years to come.

On the other side of the mountain stood huge stone Buddhas that lined the path to the peak, where the Tibetan temple stood that overlooked the surrounding area. To reach the top one had to climb three hundred sixty-five steps, with rails on either side. Before sunset every night, monkeys who had traipsed up to the temple came sliding down the rails to make their beds on the stone Buddhas, or in trees at the foot of the mountain. Quite a sight it was to see how fast the monkeys slid down and hung onto the rails. It was the monkeys' version of a waterslide park.

Tibetan monks lived in the temple on top of the mountain. They spun huge prayer wheels, praying and worshipping their vision of god. They sold Tibetan art to tourists. I became interested in the rice paper prints of their deities and of the Wheel of Life. I studied Buddhism as much as I could, because I was searching for answers to life and death. We met many young travelers who came to Nepal because of the excellent hashish, which was legal to smoke there.

Garrett and I'd spent three months in Nepal, and our relationship was fraying at the edges. He turned to me one day and said that he'd enough. I thought the same, and wanted to make it by myself. We sold the van, and I moved into an apartment and paid rent. I agreed to everything; and the time came when Garrett left Kathmandu for Hawaii where he'd been born and raised. I didn't cry over our separation but was scared to be by myself in a strange land.

ON MY OWN

What's a twenty-four-year-old woman to do alone in Nepal? I had to make money. We'd bought the van for seventy-five dollars in Ibiza and had just sold it for one hundred fifty. Garrett left me with some money to get by. I made friends and we all hung out together smoking opium. My ears were pierced using a raw potato to soften the impact of the piercing; now I could wear some of the coral and turquoise earrings the Tibetans sold. I felt sick a couple of weeks after Garrett left; I'd have nausea every morning and soon discovered that I was pregnant. I felt alone and vulnerable. I will never forget the horrific sight of a dead infant that looked as if it had just been thrown into the street; its face unrecognizable, because rats or dogs had eaten away at it; and it was just another bit of garbage discarded in the streets. It made me so sick that I knew I could never throw away a baby.

The little money I had was invested into Tibetan prints. I'd sell them to the Anglo tourists, who were flowing through *Kathmandu* like a moving stream. I met one of the Nepalese King's tailors, who spoke good English and we formed a working relationship. He had a shop in town and taught me how to make Tibetan shirts. I taught him how to make bell bottom pants. He loved his new line of trade, and provided me a small corner in his shop so that I could work with him.

The arrangement went on for a few months. Every month I would have to get my visa renewed. The first two weeks in Nepal was on an initial entry visa. I'd secured an extension while Garrett was there but now I was on my own. The usual method of getting monthly extensions was to pay an official member of the Tourist Ministry twenty dollars each time you needed an extension. The procedure was unique: after discretely paying someone, you would wait your turn in the visa office. Once inside the official's office, he would ask you what exactly you needed the visa for. I had a good reason because I now worked with an official tailor to the King. That wasn't good enough; so, for the next couple of minutes I would ritually endure official yelling and aggressive behavior; but in the end, he would stamp my passport! This went on for a total of six months; it was unusual for a westerner who was not climbing Mount Everest to stay that long in Nepal. Twenty dollars every month seemed worth it, so I obediently followed the procedure each month.

Once at a friend's house I recall saying to someone that I was so cool and that I never freaked out; and that I would remain calm in adverse situations. I immediately had to eat my words when I went to the toilet. I glanced down at my feces and saw a small, white, wiggly spaghetti-like thing emerge from the stool. The closer I looked the more frightened I became and started screaming at the top of my lungs. I had worms.

There wasn't a doctor I could visit because I didn't have insurance and couldn't afford to pay a private doctor. Someone mentioned the Peace Corps; so, I went to them and desperately begged for help to get rid of the worms. They helped me after I brought them a sample in a plastic bag, by giving me Antipar which eliminated the worms. I told them that I believed I was pregnant and didn't want anything to harm the baby. They assured me that the medication would not harm a fetus so I took it. Within a few hours, five huge worms the size of pencils were eliminated and I brought them back to the doctor.

A letter came from Garrett telling me about his time in Hawaii. Feeling alone and struggling to make ends meet, I wrote and told him I was pregnant. The next letter he sent included a marriage proposal with an offer to fly me to Hawaii. I concluded that it would be best for me and our child for us to get married, and to have the baby in Hawaii. After six months in Nepal I prepared myself for the journey which would take three days. I didn't want to return to the States empty-handed, and thought it would be a nice gift for Garrett to bring him some Nepalese hashish; and it would also help financially to sell some in Hawaii. Hiding two kilos of hash would be simple. I was used to smuggling, and had become creative in my techniques. Now I was ready for travel.

I flew through Bangkok and spent a night sleeping on the floor of the Tokyo airport. I arrived at Honolulu customs three days later. I was three months pregnant and my passport looked like a museum. Stamps from notorious drug countries filled the passport pages. I was immediately hauled into a small room and told to strip down. They did a visual body search and went through the luggage. They found nothing, but my smuggling days were now over.

OAHU

Wow, Hawaii!! What a beautiful luscious island, very different from the Mediterranean; so, green and so full of fragrant flowers everywhere you go; and beautiful, dark-skinned people who speak a pidgin Hawaiian-English which took me fifteen years to master. On a bus listening to kids talk, I wondered, what language is that? The climate was perfect. Garrett and I immediately married in downtown Honolulu.

We lived with his grandma Dot for the first month and then, as a matter of routine, Kent arrived; and was there to share the two-bedroom house we finally rented just before I gave birth to our daughter Neima. Adjusting to island living seemed easy and natural.

Kaava is on the western shore of Oahu; a sleepy little spot tucked below the mountains, surrounded by trees, and a five-minute walk to the beach. Now I was a married woman, soon to be a mother, and again experiencing life in America; although Hawaii didn't feel like the mainland of the States, living there was totally different than life in Ibiza, Morocco, Amsterdam, or India.

Our daughter was born in *Kahiku* hospital just north of *Kaava*; and I decided to live as healthily as possible. I dove headfirst into the health food lifestyle. I wanted to be a responsible mom and live as naturally as possible. I didn't want to buy food in cans and live on Franco-American spaghetti as I had growing up; it was wholesome, natural, and organic for me and my small family and that's where I directed my energies.

I walked the beaches, tanned my pregnant body, and ate from the vast, diverse supply of island fruits and vegetables at my fingertips, much of it free for the taking - coconuts, papayas, mangos, bananas, avocados, guavas; almost any tropical fruit you could imagine and in abundance.

I came across a wonderful cook book of the time called, "Ten Talents Cook Book". I cooked from and lived it, but it was more than a cook book; there were tips and hints on ways to live healthy. I soaked it all up and now was a convert to tofu.

Just one week after Neima was born the doctor discovered a heart murmur in her tiny heart. She underwent heart surgery at five months old; that was an additional strain on the relationship between Garrett and me. Emotional support and help from my husband was what I needed most with what I was dealing with. Garrett and Kent were focused instead on boats and *pakalolo* (Hawaiian for pot). I needed a stable and secure family, and thought that Kent should start his own family; but the bond between the twins was, for Garrett, thicker than the bond between his wife and baby girl.

Their first project was to build a small dinghy and practice sailing it, off the Pacific near Chinaman's Hat, near *Kaava*. The dinghy completed, we ventured out to the beach and christened the boat. Neima was then a few months old, and I thought it would be nice to watch from the shore as the two brothers set sail. They went out and came in without incident; then Garrett requested that I join him while Kent would watch Neima on the shore. I didn't want to get in the dinghy and made my sentiments clear; but steady insistence on twin fronts made it almost impossible for me to refuse. I reluctantly agreed; and let Garrett know that I would on the condition that he didn't ask me to perform any duties since I didn't know how to sail. I just wanted to sit in it, go out and come back quickly. Agreed, I kissed Neima and got into the small boat with fear and apprehension. Ask me to: drive through Arab countries, smuggle hashish, cook in and live out of a van; deal with monkeys stealing my food, but getting into that dinghy with the Mohegan freaked me out.

The water was calm and I began to feel more relaxed, when we both heard a cracking noise which caused me great anxiety. Garrett also became agitated and started to yell orders at me: grab that, hold this, move here, etcetera! I immediately froze, couldn't move, or think of anything but getting onto the shore where my baby was. The fear of being lost at sea was overpowering. I could do nothing but hang on for dear life, as Garrett jumped out of the boat while yelling orders at me. I could do nothing! Then he cut himself; now there was blood in the water and, of course, I thought of sharks. Garrett continued to hysterically freak out until we somehow managed to get back on shore; and that's where I stayed, no more to venture out in a boat with him.

After that horrific episode, I began to seriously question our marriage. I asked Garrett, again and again, what about us? Since I was prone to sea sickness, how would the twins' plan for us all to sail around the world in the 32-foot catamaran they were building realistically work? I don't remember any answers to my questions, just arguments and fights between the twins and me which occurred almost every day.

Neima was five months old now and was strong enough to undergo heart surgery at Queens Medical Center in downtown Oahu. She came through the surgery with flying colors and was now on the road to becoming healthier than she had been in the first few months of her life.

Kent was now a permanent fixture in our house and I believed that my marriage was falling apart. I made a trip to the mainland to visit Warren, and heard that a special course could help me save the marriage. I believed it was worth a try if there was a chance it would work. So, off I went and registered at the Scientology office in downtown San Francisco. Wow, that was an experience. I sat with a partner (someone I didn't know); he yelled and said things to push my buttons, and I had lots of buttons to push and I reacted. I practiced and thought that I now had some tools to work with, and so could return to Oahu and see if our marriage could be salvaged.

GUESS WHO'S ALIVE?

It was also during that time in San Francisco (Neima was about eight months old) that I visited mom and had an interesting conversation which went something like this: "Oh, guess who's alive"? I couldn't even begin to guess, so she tells me, "Your father"! (Ever since I could remember I was told that my dad was rotten, had destroyed mom's life, and that he was dead…now he was alive; hmmm, interesting!) "Do you have any idea where he might be living?" "Sure, Los Angeles." "How can I get in touch with him?" She didn't know. That night I phoned LA information; asked the operator for my father's number and, lo and behold, they had it. I called and held my breath. He answers. I say, "Hi, this is your daughter." "What do you want?" What a blow, as if I were stabbed in the heart. "I just found out from my mother that you are alive, not dead as she always told me; and after all these years not knowing that you are alive I thought I should call and let you know that you are a grandfather, that I'm married, and live in Hawaii; I'm heading back there tomorrow."

His tone changed and we ended up exchanging contact information, with the hope that one day we would get together. What I didn't know when I called was that his wife of twenty-one years was on her death bed. She had recently told my dad that his daughter would contact him. He may have been in shock when he heard my voice, and then she died a few weeks later. We kept in touch. When Neima was eighteen months old he sent me a plane ticket. I went to Los Angeles and visited him; staying for two weeks. That was a remarkable time for me and my dad. We talked and talked; that helped fill in at least some of the gaps in our family history. He had confirmed that he had visited me in the orphanage and had pictures to prove it. He took us everywhere: Disneyland, the San Diego Zoo, Palm Springs, and Mexico. We couldn't catch up on all the lost years in two weeks and would continue our relationship up until my father's death, may he rest in peace, in 1989.

Mother was furious to find out that not only had I truly found and met my dad, but that he and I actually enjoyed each other's company. She vociferously informed me that he was the devil and so, I responded, that makes me part devil! The advancing relationship with my resurrected father prompted mom to pack up and leave San Francisco and head to - you guessed it – Hawaii! She was now a card-carrying member of AA; they had clubs everywhere. She found a place to live in downtown Waikiki; around the same time that Garrett and Kent decided it was time to get more land on which to build their boat; so, we all moved to the leeward side of Oahu to *Makaha* valley. We rented a large three-bedroom house. and the twins bought a set of blueprints for building their catamaran. Our huge backyard became a shipyard. Fiberglass fumes and wood were everywhere.

My life with the twins became increasingly exhausting and rough; and I felt as if I were being pushed out of my own home. No provision was made by Garrett for me and our baby daughter. We argued all the time, and Garrett took Kent's side in everything. I tried the Scientology method with no result, and we even went to a few Baha'i meetings, in vain hope that some of their aspirations for peace and love would rub off. It got awfully aggressive, to the point of me being told to leave or else! I didn't want to risk testing a last violent episode; so, I took Neima and went to visit a friend, another single mom, who lived on the island of Hawaii (the biggest of the Hawaiian Islands). I was now alone with a toddler - a daunting proposition; not knowing what to do or where to go. There was never a penny of financial help from Garrett, so I applied for and got public assistance.

HAWAII

The Big Island is very different from Oahu; it's not heavily touristy and has more of the natural life style you might imagine when you think: Hawaii! My friend Judith, the other single mom, lived near *Kona* with her daughter. At first it was okay, but we really didn't hit it off and I didn't know anyone else. One day I went to the shore and soon realized it was a nude beach; getting ready to leave I met Jonah, an Australian. He invited me to visit the commune of hippies where he lived that might, he said, have space for me and my daughter.

So, I made the trek to Rock Bottom Road in *Kealakekua,* Hawaii. The people there were friendly, spacey, and laid back. They had claimed a spot off the road where they'd built bamboo shelters. Very primitive, there were no doors or windows, all of it was open. The tropical weather made viable such a style of life; everyone walked around, with barely any clothes on, barefoot. All the food was from the land and mostly eaten raw. Lots of *pakalolo* got smoked, which they grew themselves. The group accepted my daughter and me right away; they thought I was groovy because of all the places I had lived. So, I fit in and started to feel comfortable. My knowledge of tropical foods and natural living increased. I learned about herbal remedies and reflexology; my love for nature grew. I bought another treadle sewing machine, and even though I hardly wore any clothes, sewed all kinds of clothes for people; and also, learned how to crochet. Life was mellow; the only disturbances were mosquitoes and the local missionaries who would come and talk to us; and try to convince us that we were sinners and needed to repent. I usually escaped into the bushes during their periodic visits.

I spent months in the commune with lots of interesting characters. There were, though, frightening experiences in the water. There was a little cove down by the *Green Sand* beach. I went out swimming one day, and was warned to be careful because the current was strong; it could take you out in a moment. I stayed close to shore and, nevertheless, got pulled out to sea. I tried hard to swim back, but the current was intense and my swimming skills aren't strong. I yelled for help and a man on a surfboard pulled me in.

I no longer had the need to prove I could be an accomplished sea-faring woman; I've been a landlubber ever since. I love the beach and love to sit by the water and dip my toes in but that's about it.

Six months on, Neima and I were nicely living down Rock Bottom Road. I got good at crocheting bathing suits while sitting on the sand, and selling them to tourists. A friend of someone in the commune had just come back from a trip to Maui. He described a land deal in development in the secluded town of *Hana*; where virgin rain forest property was available at very low prices to people able to put down a minimal amount of money. If we pooled our money we'd have enough for a deposit and go into the deal as partners. We'd be able to build our own dwellings and beautifully live on a mountain top. The trusting, naïve person I was then happily put in the two thousand dollars I'd saved; and off to the island of Maui trekked our Real Estate Investment in Paradise Group.

MAUI NO KA OI

Maui no ka *oi* means '*Maui* is the best'; and in many ways *Maui* is the best of the Hawaiian islands. In 1974, to reach the incredible place on earth called *Hana* one had to travel for more than two hours on a very long and narrow, winding road that crossed over fifty-two bridges and fifty-two waterfalls; all the while dodging potholes and hugging the mountain side; with the ever-present danger of huge boulders falling onto your car and crushing you to death.

We five intrepid communal cohorts traveled to *Hana* to view our land; it was quite a journey. Once there we made our way up the mountain to the first section of the property. A dirt road had already been bulldozed, but we couldn't take our car up to where we had to go. I hadn't asked too many questions about the living conditions we'd face; I felt that it was all somehow being taken care of.

Hana is on the rainy side of Maui, which means that things get wet. Even though the Hawaiian Islands are warm, it was still hard to get used to the continual moisture and damp. Some of the land was already inhabited by others, commercially growing papayas. Our stretch lay further up the mountain. So, we hoofed it for another ten minutes and there it was: tropical virgin rain forest, nothing but the lush, green foliage of trees in a thick jungle! We now had to figure out how we were actually going to live there – without any structures, plumbing, water, or electricity.

LIVING ON THE LAND

We bought supplies. I got myself a machete, and we all started cutting back the forest. Up went a lean-to of guava posts and plastic sheeting, for protection from the rain. Large rain barrels, strategically placed under plastic roofing, caught the daily rainwater. A bucket served nicely as a toilet, until we built an outhouse of sorts. Grass mats went down on the dirt floors and futons were our beds. We all slept together. At night, rats from the jungle would jump on our heads and bounce off. They weren't little furry creatures, but big jungle rats. Not pleasant! Cooking was on wood fires; we ran around naked half the time because clothes were cumbersome in that kind of weather. I developed really tough feet; walking barefoot up and down the mountain carrying heavy loads.

I was a single mom with a two-and-a-half-year-old daughter, and began to think that living all together with the guys was not the best environment for her. I decided to build my own shelter down the trail - to do my own thing, but still be part of the commune. The group didn't take it very well; nonetheless I took my machete and started to clear a trail, having located a good spot in the thick tropical brush. It wasn't easy, but I was quite strong then and had the resolve to make my own shelter.

Some of us took time off to go on a three-day trek through *Haleakala* Crater, one of the most fascinating dormant volcanoes in the world. Located at the top of Maui, it is ten thousand feet high, with a deep crater noted for its rich natural diversity. Rainbow and Patchouli, an older hippie couple with a daughter Neima's age, babysat while the group of us got a ride north and headed down into the crater. Everyone else wore sandals or shoes; I barefooted it because I wanted to *feel* the crater. I hiked for three days over rocks, dirt, gravel, and sheer, razor sharp lava rocks; up and down switchbacks, over lunar landscapes, and saw the silver sword plants in full bloom. Hiking down the back side, leading to the eastern *Kipahulu* side of Maui, from barren landscape to lush waterfalls, my feet experienced it all! I hitched a ride back to the land with a couple of people staying on the property who worked the papaya fields.

HUSBAND NUMBER TWO

One of them was Stanley. He had just arrived from Alaska and boy was he white! We struck up a conversation; perhaps because he was impressed by my ability to hike barefoot. When he discovered that I was one of the partners, who lived up the road from the main facility, and was building my own shelter, he volunteered to help me clear the land and construct something simple.

We worked together to put up a twenty by twenty-foot wooden platform in a clearing off the dirt road; a living space for me and my daughter. I put a tent on it to keep the rats out. That was the beginning of the end of my partnership with the commune. They didn't like that I was independent, had my own living space; plus, now I had help, which infuriated them to the point that they asked me to leave. Okay; so, where's the money I invested; what money; what investment? I didn't want trouble, even though I could see it coming for months. I left peaceably with Neima and Stanley. We found somewhere to live in *Hana* town and never looked back. Eventually, everyone on the mountain lost their stake in the land and had to move.

LITTLE VALLEY

We were a couple now and I was pregnant with Stanley's baby. Fortunately, Stanley got along with Neima; it seemed that he was a good role model for her. It was hard for Stan to find work in *Hana*; and a friend of his from  Alaska invited us to Little Valley, California. We left beautiful *Hana*; and with Neima in tow, rented a small two-bedroom wooden cabin in northern California; where Stan began to trap and hunt coyotes in the surrounding woods. We kept in touch with a *haoli* couple, Frances and Puka John, who had property in the jungle of *Hana*, in *Ulaino*. *Haoli* is a very interesting word; its meaning depends on how it's used. *Without the breath of God* is how it was explained to me. When the island people saw, Captain Cook they called him *Haoli*. The locals call any white person, *Haoli*; usually in a derogatory way as in, "you *Haoli* trash!" Frances and Puka John had moved to  California, and didn't have anyone to take care of the home they'd constructed in *Ulaino*. They heard we were in California but missing *Hana*; and not making any real money trapping, and selling coyote pelts.

We lived in Little Valley for six months. I gave birth to my second daughter, Sidra, there at home in candlelight;

there was no midwife (Stanley delivered her), and the cabin was heated with a wood burning stove. Labor lasted four hours, Stanley cut the cord, and we buried the placenta under a tree. Sid weighed nine and a half pounds, and I didn't see a doctor until she was a week old.

We gladly accepted the offer to move back to *Hana*; and became caretakers for the Jungle House; so back to Maui went Stan and me, with Neima and a one month old baby in tow.

ULAINO

Hana **is considered** the, "last Hawaiian place", while *Ulaino* is a world in itself. Turn off the main *Hana* highway and drive down a single lane dirt road for about two miles before you reach the actual town of *Hana*. Then pass over two riverbeds (the foliage gets thicker the further down the road you go). Almost at the end of the road is a turnoff that leads to a two-story wooden structure without electricity or running water; but there are mongooses and mosquitoes, and no glass to cover openings in the walls for windows. When we arrived with

 Neima, aged four and Sidra, just over two months old, I had no idea about what kind of life we'd be living over the next four years. The house was rent free; because Frances and Puka John in California needed someone to inhabit it. We became caretakers, and moved into our new home in *Ulaino*. Setting up house, I could hardly believe our surroundings: the jungle was rapidly taking over; vines and shrubbery grew inside the house, only a couple of months since no one had lived there. The front door had no lock; which didn't much matter, since anyone could climb through any of the empty spaces that served as windows. Everything was open. Hawaiian weather in that specific spot meant that you didn't get cold because *Ulaino* was on the ocean side. We didn't get the mountain air and harsher weather, but still had the almost daily rain showers. The house was sheltered by many trees: mangos, avocados, bananas, mountain apples, coconut, guavas, and breadfruit; even coffee bushes grew

there. Nearby, waves crashed on the rocks at the shore; and in heavy rains, roaring in the near distance, you could hear a waterfall rushing into our next-door neighbor's riverbed.

But, how are we to keep mosquitoes away from the kids; and other insects, rodents, and wildlife out of the house?

 Where do we get water when there's no rain? How do we cook and keep food fresh? How do we clean our clothes, take baths, and where do we go when we have to go to the toilet? All relatively simple questions to ask and answer - living it was the challenge!

Our Jungle house had a kitchen sink with a hand pump; it drew water from a fifty-five-gallon drum outside, which would collect rain water runoff from the massive tin roof. Mosquito punk coils were lighted during the day throughout the house. At night, we would crawl into our

 beds under mosquito netting, hoping that the big red ants, centipedes, geckos, flying cockroaches and other critters always around, didn't crawl into our beds and bite us. We had a post bed; would fill up dishes with water, and place the posts of the bed inside the dishes. Then we'd wrap masking tape, sticky side out, around the posts; which acted as an effective moat to deter the ants. They didn't like to cross the water; and if they did get across then they had to deal with the sticky stuff. We discovered how

important it was to have cats; they ate rats, bugs, and our leftovers; geckos ate the mosquitos.

Aargh; the outhouse! Exit the kitchen to the back porch, cross over the lava rock trail to enter the jungle outhouse: a cozy one person built-to purpose shelter; not too private but private enough. A deep hole had been dug, I presume, by Puka John; lime powder was thrown onto the pile to keep the smell and flies down. It was messy getting to and from it during rainstorms but we managed.

The kitchen had a gas stove, with two small propane tanks, filled in town when they were empty; at least we didn't have to use wood to cook our food. The tanks would last about a month or two. There was no refrigeration but we had a medium size Coleman's cooler that would fit a block of ice; that would keep things cool for two or three days if we didn't open it too often. The  nearest place to replace ice blocks was in town; about a twenty-minute ride on the jungle road. Or one could hike over the first riverbed; go up the mountain through more jungle and up, finally, to the main *Hana* road to hitch a ride into town. Then, back again, hike down through the jungle with the block of ice before it melted! The trek took a couple of hours; sometimes I would do it with a baby strapped to my back; or like the Nepalese women did, with a piece of material to strap the baby to my side, and keep her on me like that. I never owned a baby carriage.

Bathing was a fascinating experience: when the weather was hot and there was enough water, a second fifty-five-gallon drum was positioned near the back porch. Exposed to the sun, you could stand under the shower drum with a spigot, and take a short shower with relatively warm water. That was good for us adults; but for a four-year-

old and a toddler it didn't work. We had, though, a huge tin bucket called a *pakini*. I would heat water in a pot on the stove and pour it, along with some cold water, into the *pakini* and give the kids a bucket bath. They got used to it, and I tried to make it a fun time. When there wasn't enough water, we would all trek to the riverbed by the ocean.

BLUE POND

Life in *Ulaino* was both challenging and exciting. A good part of life there consisted of being down by the water a good deal of the time, almost as much as being in the jungle house. Past the entrance to our home, located at the very end of the *Ulaino* road was the ocean. Coming out of the jungle into a clearing and onto the boulder beach, was a breathtaking view of the Pacific Ocean, in all its wonder and force. If you climbed over the huge boulders, and ventured onto even larger ones, you would see one of the most beautiful sights that creation offers us, a secluded place called Blue Pond. Only the locals knew it; and only someone just exploring would be able to find it. The waterfall at Blue Pond is at least one hundred feet high and is set back about forty feet from the ocean. Blue Pond was my solace, the place I could commune with God. I was all alone, so I would talk to Him and cry, pray, sing, and laugh, and no one would hear or see me. The pond was invitingly shaped: round and deep in certain areas, and easy to slide or dive into. I would swim up to the waterfall, and crawl behind the heavy force of cascading water. I'd sit there, and look out from behind the sheet of water at the world as if in a perfect dream of Shangri-La! The water was cold but refreshing; and on a hot day both delightful and invigorating. Maidenhair ferns grew from the walls of the pond; and many varieties of tropical foliage were there in abundance, even the 'shampoo ginger' I would use to wash my hair. On days alone without the kids, I would swim there and lay out on one of the biggest boulders. I would sun my body, close my eyes, and listen to the roar of the ocean on one side and the peaceful sound of the waterfall on the other. I would gaze at the blue water of the pond, at the black craggy seashore, and at the ocean and lush jungle foliage. I knew that paradise wasn't far away. Smoking *pakalolo* helped to heighten my senses; I knew though, that it was the fantastic location which helped me commune with myself and with God. Sometimes my mind would drift back to when I was a small kid; when I wished, my life was better, when I'd make deals with God to get me out of the hell hole with our mother.

Before reaching Blue Pond, one of the locals in *Ulaino* had put a PVC pipe into the mountain wall and out came fresh water. It came from way up the mountain side and gushed non-stop, even in the heaviest of droughts, and never ran dry. Locals also planted watercress there. The spout made it easy to fill up our ten-gallon water container, strap it to our backs, and haul it back to the jungle house. I would also haul the *pakini* down to the pipe and do my laundry there beside the watercress. The kids would play on the rocks and boulders as I would hand wash our clothes. There were no plastic diapers in the 1970s, or at least I'd not heard of them; I used cloth ones; even if there had been a diaper service in *Hana* I wouldn't have used it. I'd lay our clean clothes all over the rocks and boulders, and the sun would dry them while the kids played and sometimes took naps on the boulders. When there was no water available in the jungle house, I would haul dirty dishes as well down to the pipe and wash them in the *pakini*.

Washing one day and napping, I noticed that the waves were getting bigger and closer to us on the rocks. I moved everyone further back. The waves got even bigger and closer. One wave came in suddenly and almost washed away the *pakini* and our clothes. I grabbed the girls, and ran to the jungle clearing where we watched as a big storm hit.

It would rain almost every day in *Hana* during the rainy times, but it would quickly come and go. Living in a rain forest jungle we had to adapt to the constant humidity. After a while everything was mildewed. Our clothes and bedding always smelled musty. Everything that needed to stay dry, such as matches and envelopes, would be kept in air tight containers. Food also had to be kept dry and out of the reach of not so friendly little critters, such as the mongoose. Mongooses were everywhere on the *Hana* side of Maui. They'd been introduced to the island many years before in order to eat rats; but someone neglected to realize that mongooses are not nocturnal; the rats and mongooses never met each other! They are good little thieves, and would come into the jungle house through all the openings and steal whatever food they would find. We had to hide fresh food under bowls and buckets. I once visited an elderly Hawaiian man who lived on the outskirts of *Hana*. He lived by himself but shared his dwelling with the mongooses. When you entered his shelter, there were mongooses running in and out, and he hid food under all kinds of containers. It was amazing to see how mongooses had such freedom of movement in someone's home. We had a large vegetable garden in *Ulaino,* as well as six chickens. They laid eggs that the mongooses would steal and eat. There was almost every conceivable fruit available; and between the fresh fish, the vegetables and fruit, we had very little else to buy.

COCONUTS

We didn't work and collected welfare. I was a stay at home jungle mom; and did the cooking, washing, and gardening, and would make my own coconut milk. I was quite good with the machete and could husk a fresh coconut off a tree. The hard shell surrounding a coconut is ready when brown. The husk needs to be stripped away from the coconut inside. The fiber of the coconut husk is very tough and hard to separate from the coconut meat; but I was good at it, and during a 'fun day' in *Hana* town I almost won a competition for fast female huskers. I'd husk the coconut, then crack the brown, hairy shell in two to find the white meat inside. Stan fashioned a car spring with jagged edges resembling a saw blade. The spring was positioned between two pieces of wood I was able to sit on and hold down with my body. Sitting on the back-

porch steps, I'd hold half a coconut up to the jagged saw, and scrape the inside white meat into a bowl. After I'd shredded two or three coconuts, which took about twenty minutes, I poured water onto the shredded meat, then scooped up the wet coconut and squeezed out the coconut milk into another bowl. I repeated the process with the dried, squeezed, shredded coconut and had rich, creamy coconut milk that the kids would drink and I would cook with; yummy!

My all-time favorite jungle recipe is

Breadfruit boiled in freshly squeezed coconut milk
Cut up one fresh breadfruit into small cubes...Cover with coconut milk and boil until the milk evaporates and saturates the breadfruit. Then slightly brown the breadfruit in the pot until almost toasted...BROKE DA MOTH! Hawaiian for delicious.

I even had my treadle sewing machine, and can modestly claim that I probably had the strongest ankles in the jungle (there were only five families living down in *Ulaino*, we were the only *Haolis* at the time, the rest were pure Hawaiian locals). I was sewing clothes for the girls and making cowboy shirts for men. I would sell the shirts to boutiques on the other side of the island, or in *Lahaina* on the west side of Maui. I needed a label to put into my creations and since my birth name is Suzanne, I took the Zanne and Zig Zag Zanne became my label. On one of my hikes up the mountain into town, I met another *Haoli* couple. They lived in a wooden structure and had electricity; we became friends. Rochelle was an artist and clothes designer. She'd design lovely island-inspired silk creations and I sewed them; that worked out well, and we've stayed friends over the years, even after I left the islands. Rochelle is now a famous artist on Maui.

After about a year in the jungle house I was pregnant again, with my third child. Since I had successfully given birth to Sidra at home in Little Valley, I wanted to birth this child at home as well, though it was more complicated without running water or electricity! There were kerosene lanterns and candles, and we knew what it took to deliver a baby; but it was still a twenty-minute drive to the local medical center. If the riverbeds were flooded we wouldn't be able to make it, so we had better be prepared to have a home birth. We invested in some heavy-duty plastic sheeting to cover some of the house's open spaces and better protect us from the elements. All the openings couldn't be sealed because then it would feel like we were living in a plastic house. I liked having fresh air all the time. The big storm of 1978, though, made me anxious about our living conditions.

JUNGLE BIRTH

I was nine months pregnant and due at any time. Every week Stanley would go into town or to the other side of the island and buy supplies. Since I was so close to delivering my child I thought that he'd better go sooner rather than later. That way we would be ready if the baby came within the next week or so. He took our old Volkswagen van; we'd gone through three VW vans, living down in *Ulaino* and driving on the *Hana* highway to *Kahului*; it was only forty miles away, but took a couple of hours to navigate the winding, pothole ridden road. Stan took Neima with him, and I stayed at home with Sidra, who was two. A big rainstorm occurred while they were gone. Usually after a rainstorm, there is flooding in the riverbeds where waterfalls flow. This time there was unusual flooding; and the second river bed was so swollen with rushing water that when Stanley and Neima returned from the other side they couldn't cross over for nine hours. Meantime, Sidra and I huddled in a corner of her room trying to stay dry as the rain stormed into the jungle house and got everything wet. There, with her, I dreaded the thought of delivering the baby at home in those conditions. The possibility frightened me but I thought, if I had to I would. After nine hours passed, Stanley and Neima came home from the other side of the river bed, and Gema was born a few days later.

This home birth was an incredible experience. I had enjoyed the natural birth of Sidra, but this was different. Stan and I played cribbage late that night; and the kids were asleep. I felt the contractions start at around midnight. Our bed was on the second level loft area. Sometimes, to avoid climbing down steep stairs to the first level, and then go outside climb over the lava rocks to the outhouse, Stan would urinate into the jungle below. I usually objected and would send him to the outhouse since the smell was unpleasant. As the contractions became stronger I knew it was time; Stan had an urge to pee so he started heading down to go outside, this time I relented and out the window it went.

PLACENTA, IT'S GOOD FOR YOU!

The birthing pack was already; we'd sterilized it in the gas oven and were ready for our baby to arrive. A mere two hours of labor later, Gema almost effortlessly slid out and was welcomed into the world - all ten pounds of her! Stan didn't cut the umbilical cord until hours later; and we presented Gema to her two sisters in the morning when they awoke. The placenta was delivered as with Sidra's birth; but this time, instead of burying it under a tree, we did something different with the afterbirth. *(At this point in the story you may want to skip this part, especially if you have a weak stomach.)*

Stan had read in several natural birthing books that eating the placenta just after giving birth was good for the health of the mother. I wasn't overjoyed at the prospect but was

exhausted. Stan insisted the next morning that I try it. Hearing him downstairs fry up the fully intact remnants of the night before, with heavenly aromas from the sautéing potatoes, garlic, and onions I began to get hungry. Weird and a bit bizarre, how will I ever tell my child that I ate her placenta? Gema has by now heard the story so many times that she doesn't think twice about it. Yup; there I was, hungrily downing placenta stir fry; although I don't recommend Stan's recipe, I must admit that I was up on my feet almost instantly – ten minutes later! - out in the garden picking vegetables. We took our baby to the medical center a few days later; Dr. Howell was not happy to see me with a newborn. I told him that she was born within two hours of my contractions; and that there was no time to rush from the jungle into town in the middle of the night with two sleepy kids.

ALOHA PAKALOLO & JUNGLE LIVING

I remember my last experience with *pakalolo*. I was hiking down the mountain with some supplies and stopped to say hello to a fellow jungle neighbor along the way. We were sitting around and she offered me some cookies to eat. I ate one or two and went on my way. By the time I arrived home I was high. How did that happen and why wouldn't someone tell me that the cookies were loaded with pot? I remembered the wedding experience on the island of Formentera. Then there was Bill, who would play an important role in our lives.

Stan and I had met Bill in *Hana* town and we all hit it off. Bill had come to Maui from Los Angeles to get away from it all and to lead a spiritual life. He needed to find a calm space where he could meditate; he'd rented a three-bedroom house in *Hana* town, and was looking for something more remote. Bill moved to the jungle house and we took over the rented three-bedroom house in town. The move went smoothly and we developed a good relationship with our new landlords, Ted and Zelly. Bill liked the jungle and we all got along. We were cleaned up and more respectable now and needed to move up and out of the jungle. We needed to send Neima to school and now was the time for change.

HANA

Our new house was only a ten-minute walk to *Hana* Bay. There was enough land in the back to plant a substantial garden; and with electricity I was able to use an electric sewing machine. Now all we needed to do was come up with the rent every month. Behind the house was a small cabin that slept up to six people. Ted and Zelly would sometimes come and stay there on the weekends. They asked if we wanted to exchange rent for helping them rent out the *Kauwiki* cabin, as it was called, to tourists. Why not? It couldn't be that hard. We had a

washing machine in the carport to wash cabin bedding; and a phone so we could easily take reservations from Zelly. After a couple of months another neighbor asked if we could do the same and manage their home down the street. This was a real job and we were making real money. A few months later an owner of a home sited right on *Hana* Bay hired us to do the same thing.

Within a year, we had five properties to manage. I fondly remember the day I phoned the Welfare Department, and thanked them for all the help they had given us over the years. Now we were off the Welfare rolls; staff there said that never before had anyone leave Welfare so graciously; it gave me such satisfaction and happiness to realize that level of accomplishment; looking back at the years of growing up on Welfare.

The move from jungle to town was liberating. Our big orange tom cat, OJ, made the journey with us. He quickly adapted to small town living. OJ was my buddy. When we lived in the jungle, I would call OJ if I saw a rat in the house. He would come and sit where I pointed and wait patiently until he caught it. What he loved more than catching rats though, was to torture the dogs living next to our new home in town. Our big, orange tom would venture out into the cul-de-sac near our house and sit in the road like he owned it. Next you we'd hear barking and growling from a dog; then silence, and the eventual whelping from the injured canine, whose nose OJ would have

scratched. The dogs would invariably flee the scene of battle, leaving the field to the victorious cat, who preened himself serenely unaffected by their plight.

Living in *Hana* town opened up many opportunities for my involvement in community activities. Under the auspices of the 4H club I taught young girls how to sew. Still hanging in the local school library, *Hana* Medical

Center, and Senior Citizens building, are lovely artworks the kids created.

Hana Bay Vacation Rentals was the name for our property management business, and what a business it was: I handled reservations, collected and deposited money, cleaned, bought supplies, and sometimes decorated the homes. Stanley was Mr. Fixit and could repair almost anything. He would haul the trash and mow the lawns. Most of our business came through word of mouth. When Frommer's included us in their Maui Travel Guide, and an article in the LA Times Travel Section featured us, our *Hana* Bay business kept us very busy indeed. We had to turn down requests to take on new homes to manage. Stan and I met so many interesting people then, but it would be a blue-tiled-roof home on *Hana* Bay that would by far attract the most interesting guests.

FLOWERS FROM GEORGE

In the ocean front of *Hana* was a huge, custom-built house with a vivid blue tile roof that makes the property stand out from the other homes nearby. An agent called and wanted to rent the house for his clients, but was unwilling to reveal their identity. Unless we knew who, they were, I told him, we would not be able to lease to his clients. Round and around went the 'pin the identity on the secret client game'; I stood my ground and won in the end. Former Beatle George Harrison and his family would stay in the house while waiting for their new home to be completed on sixty acres they had purchased in lower *Nahiku,* several miles from *Hana.*

The day came to go over and meet the Harrisons. I was excited; although I rarely hold celebrities on too high a pedestal. I'd realized early on that we're all equal, even though some of us are a bit more equal than others. After introductions, I hit it off immediately with Olivia, George's wife. Their son Danny, his nanny, and George's bodyguard all stayed in the house. I explained the house's logistics; and was friendly, but not too friendly at first. Visits to the house were frequent and we became friends. Friendship with the Harrisons is a special part of my life and for the sake of privacy, there are certain details I will not share.

However, one night we went over to visit them and Stanley made pizza, which went down well, both the pizza and the visit. By the time their home was finished, we had established a nice friendship, as well as a suitable working relationship. There were serious conversations; especially when George would talk about his security concerns after the assassination of John Lennon. There was trust between us. When George and Livia were ready to move into their *Nahiku* home, I helped them clean it up for habitation. They would call me when coming to town, and ask me to buy and stock their house with groceries. We all ate health foods so it was very easy to shop for them.

Once after getting out of my car at the Hasegawa General Store, the local all-purpose meeting place; in front of the store I saw George sitting in the driver's seat of his 4-wheel drive Land Rover. He saw me and I went over; we gave each other a hug and little cheek pecks and said our hellos. He said that Livia was in the store with Danny; so, I went in and found them in the midst of the store's usual crowded chaos. When talking with Livia, a strange woman came up to us, interrupted, and asked if I knew whether the person sitting in the car outside was a Beatle? I innocently replied, "What's a Beatle"? Livia and I gave each other "the look"! We quickly said our goodbyes before there was a scene. George really liked his privacy. That was evident when looking at the design of the homes he had built on the sixty acres he'd purchased; and the way the two attached Polynesian houses were situated far from the entrance to the property. The dirt road leading to their house was off a paved road, off the main *Hana* highway, and was itself hard to find. Star chasers would do their utmost to get a peek; even tour helicopters flew as close as possible to get a glimpse of the famous Beatle and his family.

Even though we lived in *paradise*, Stanley and I had marital problems; we had a rough thirteen years together. The first years were good: we were stoned and living in the jungle. It was when I decided to quit drugs and lead a respectable, sober life that the going got rough! Stan deserted me and the kids three times in the years we were married. He'd take all the money out of our bank account and disappear! I was left with the property management business and the kids in a small town of under two thousand people. They knew what was going on, and that didn't make it easier.

During one of those episodes, I went to the only post office in *Hana*. Here's a mental picture of what the town of *Hana* was like in the 1980s: one road in and out of town, rolling hills and fields filled with thousands of grazing cattle, one hotel, no traffic lights, a couple of stop signs, a small Medical center, two grocery stores, one gas station, one baseball field, one school for grades K-12, and a bank that opened from 3 – 4:30pm. The High School math teacher would rush - well no one really rushed - from school to be at the bank in order to open it up on time for the customers. Next to the bank was the post office, with all the mail boxes on the outside walls of the building. You could write to someone in *Hana* without knowing their box number. Amy, the post office lady, would put it in their box because she knew everyone. If you wanted to see someone, and you didn't know how to get in touch with them, all you had to do was wait outside the post office and before long they would come by to check their mail.

One of the days Stan was gone I was feeling down; balancing the business, the kids, and trying to keep on a happy face. I was checking the mail and Amy said to wait; that she had a big box for me. I thought, *yeah right* but waited. She put a huge box of flowers on the window sill. My eyes must have bulged out of my head when I read the card, "To Suzanne, we're thinking about you and thought these would cheer you up, love George." That made my day, lifting me out of the doldrums; especially when I opened the box to view the most exotically beautiful and expensive blooms *Hana* had to offer. Back home I arranged them in a huge vase; and made those flowers last as long as I could. I will always remember the kindness George showed me with such a gift, when I needed it most, and his sweet accompanying note!

It was George's birthday and I knew that he was interested in Eastern religions. I still had the beautiful little painting from Dharmsala, India; painted by one of the Dalai Lama's artist monks. I gave it to George as a gift; which I know that he appreciated. It was too difficult for me, though, at that stage to continue going to the Harrisons. They needed a caretaker to watch over their entire property; and had built a private two-bedroom home for that purpose. We had been asked; but with Stanley's instability and inconstancy, and taking care of all our other customers from *Hana* Bay Vacation Rentals, we weren't up to doing the job. So, the Harrisons hired a couple, with whom we became friends. Darlene and Steve were our age, and their daughter was the same age as our youngest daughter. We would visit each other all the time, up until the day I left *Hana* with the girls in 1988.

Hana was an incredible place to live. I have pleasant memories of all the projects I was involved with, especially ones related to tofu! I ate, cooked, and authored articles about tofu in the local *Hana* paper. I made fresh tofu from scratch; and taught others how to make fresh tofu, and how to cook with it. One semester I taught a class on tofu at the Maui Community College; and also gave classes to the locals, and to the hippie *haolis* who loved all the natural back to earth stuff. My basic texts were the Ten Talents Cook Book and Back to Eden. I've added others but those two were my favorites. I concocted so many recipes with tofu, that the name *Tofu Sue* stuck. The kids' favorite was my

Tofu Meatloaf

Mash firm fresh tofu in a bowl. Add chopped onion, rolled oats, herbs, salt, paprika, ginger, turmeric, and chopped parsley. Mix everything together with your hands and place in an oiled casserole dish. Pat down the mixture and shape if necessary into a loaf. Cover and place in the oven on about 350 degrees and bake until the loaf turns brown, but not burnt. Use around one to two packages of firm tofu per recipe. Serve hot as a main dish with mashed potatoes, or cold in a sandwich.

When we lived in town I created everything to eat from scratch: I made our own mayonnaise and bean sprouts, and always had a huge garden from which came all our fresh salads and vegetables. There was always a whole

stalk or two of bananas hanging on our *lanai* (porch); so I would make banana bread, dried bananas, banana ice cream, banana jam, and:

Chocolate Covered Frozen Bananas

Peel ripe bananas and cut into 3 to 4 rounds, depending on the size of the banana. Take wooden popsicle sticks and insert into each round section of the banana and place on a tray covered with wax paper into the freezer. When frozen solid, melt chocolate of your choice in a double boiler or microwave and dip each frozen banana into the melted chocolate. For variety, you can then dip the chocolate banana into chopped nuts or coconut. Place back in the freezer. When everything has set, then you can store the frozen treats into zip lock bags in the freezer, but a warning....The shelf life is very short...everyone will eat them up quickly!

The results from keeping our Champion Juicer happy were an inexhaustible supply of fresh fruit juices from all the local fruits available such as passion fruit. Whatever I couldn't use right away I would puree; then put them into ice cube trays to freeze; and then I'd use the cubes for smoothies. I'd make nut milks that the kids didn't like to drink. The truth came out years later, about how much they didn't like nut milk; but I thought, and still think, that they were delicious.

Sewing continued and ramped up. Now that I was living in town with power, I had an electric sewing machine. I was sewing all the time and made the girls all their clothes. My specialty was men's cowboy shirts. I couldn't make them fast enough for the boutiques on the other side of the island.

We had a wonderful cockatiel bird named *KoKo* and at times I would clip her wings so she couldn't fly but it was this one time that I let her wings grow out and she would fly around the house...Hawaiian breezes would flow  through our 3-bedroom house on *Kauwiki* St. and this one time she had landed on one of the bedroom doors and the wind slammed the door shut on her tiny leg. When I got to her she was traumatized and her right leg was hanging...I was anticipating amputating it with scissors but then thought maybe our local *Hana* Medical Center could do it better. So I wrapped *KoKo* up in a towel and drove the 3 mins to the Medical Center and one of the local doctors on staff was there…Unfortunately, there was no veterinarian in *Hana* and the closest was on the 'other side', about a two hour drive...I didn't think poor little *KoKo* could make it, let alone me. So, I asked the doctor if he could amputate her leg and he said to wait a minute. He called the vet on the other side and then we went into the 'operating room'. He laid *KoKo* on her back, face up on the stainless-steel table with the huge bright light over his little feathered patient. The vet had told him to line up her hanging limb with her other leg (both the width of a toothpick) and once lined up, then take some scotch tape and wrap it around like a splint. We went back and I made her comfortable in the bottom of her cage, anticipating her broken leg to turn black. But it never did and she eventually bit through the tape and her itty-bitty leg was healed.

We moved from the first house on *Kauwiki* Street to another house in *Hamoa* on the outskirts of *Hana*. *Hamoa* took up a small side road off the main *Hana* road, and was located at water's edge in Tsunami territory. The house was old. Local lore was that it had been located at the water's edge, near the front of a large piece of the land; but because of a tidal wave in the 1960s, it was  relocated to the back. Living and working next to the cabin in town was getting tiresome and we needed more privacy away from the business; Ted and Zelly also wanted to rent the big house to tourists since it would bring in more income; so we relocated to the *Hamoa* house. Now we had more land to garden on; and inherited twenty-five wild chickens and a Hawaiian duck we named Quack. We also got a dog we named Tubs (inspired by Miami Vice), as well as nine cats!

With all the space, I decided to commercially grow basil. I created different plots and planted basil in stages: I'd pick half the basil from one plot, then drive to *Lahaina* and sell to Italian restaurants; I'd return with about one hundred dollars, which worked out well; although the drive, which took five hours' round trip, was a killer.

It was paradise: we had a large vegetable garden with a large variety of tropical fruit trees; and lived a mere five-minute walk from one of the most beautiful beaches in the world - at least according to James Michener! *Hamoa* Beach is a truly fabulous spot on Maui. The *Hana* Hotel owned the part of the beach, to and from where they would shuttle their guests to provide food and entertainment. The beach itself is public, as are most beaches in Hawaii. I would take the girls to *Hamoa* beach all the time. We would sit, play, swim, picnic and meet with friends. Life went on like that for many years. The kids learnt to play with what was around them. They would create the most beautiful twig and sand gardens imaginable, and they enjoyed themselves. We didn't have a T.V. but an upright piano and piano lessons for all the girls.

Because most homes in *Hana*, especially in *Hamoa,* are built on stilts, the girls spent hours under the house playing. That was their space. It was also the locale for the wild chickens. We would hunt almost every day for

their eggs. Occasionally I would wrangle the chickens into the pen at the back of the house, but they always managed to escape. Want to know how to catch a chicken? I would gather a bunch of chicken feed, and put some into a little pile not far from the *lanai;* then would I make a noose with a long string of medium cording that would slide easily. The noose part I would open up and place around the chicken feed on the ground and hide some of the string with the feed; then I'd sit and wait on the *lanai* - waiting was the most exciting part. The chickens always went for the feed; and as soon as they entered the circle, I'd quickly pull the cord. Nine pulls out of ten would catch me a chicken in the noose. They would squawk and scream; I'd hold them upside down, untie the string, and take them to their pen, and put them inside. The game of chicken went on for years. It was fun and challenging, you had to be quick and precise. The girls also spent many hours on the tin roof that topped the house, below the mango tree, from which they ate their fill of mangos.

We had so many animals, and situations involving animals, that at times I felt like a real farm wife. There were names for them all: Harry and Mary were our rooster and his favorite hen; OJ our orange tomcat from the jungle house; Tubs our Irish Setter/Lab mix; *Keiki* our cockatiel; mama kitty; sister kitty; gray kitty; and of course, Quack the duck, who came with the house. He was a mean duck, and would attack almost everyone who came onto the property. I'd have to run out with my broom and chase Quack away so that he wouldn't terrorize guests. Stan's mom, grandma Ruby, was there for a visit and was sitting on the *lanai*; she called me outside and asked if I had ever seen a cow with a bucket on its head. Near the yard in the driveway, sure enough, was a small cow meandering with a bucket over its head. I went over and tried to get it off with my broomstick, but couldn't; somehow the poor creature found its way onto the road again.

Once Tubs and I went for an early morning walk down *Hamoa* road and a jogger came towards us. Tubs, was a friendly dog and, in greeting, jumped on the jogger who turned out to be Kris Kristofferson. I apologized and off he went on his morning run. Many celebrities bought property in *Hana* during those years: Jim Nabors, Eddie Albert, and Richard Pryor to name only a few of the rich and famous, who believed they could live relatively quiet lives away from the hustle and bustle of stardom in our little town. One lovely lady who rented a home from us was Julie Newmar, the original Cat Woman.

Once, while living in *Hamoa,* there was an earthquake in Alaska; which triggered a tsunami warning for the Hawaiian Islands. Helicopters flew over *Hana*, and police came down the road giving residents two hours to pack up what they could take with them and leave. We had two vehicles: a pickup truck and a seven-passenger van. I packed clothes and documents; the dog, cats, bird; and things I thought we would need if everything was lost in a tidal wave. The chickens were let loose, but Quack was nowhere to be found. We drove to *Hana* town, which was out of the tsunami area. We had friends who lived up the mountain, went up there, and got a bird's eye view of the ocean and what was happening. Thank God nothing happened; except that I had to trap a lot of chickens when I returned.

It was all about community life. I was the only Jew in town, at least that I knew of. There were many churches in town, and a mixture of local native Hawaiians and *Haolis.* I believe that I was accepted, even though a *Haoli,* while I lived there. I continued to sew and manage the *Hana* Bay Vacation Rentals. At the age of forty I got my Real Estate License, and started to work with the Hana Land Company.

In 1987 my dad, may his soul be at peace, knowing that he had a good relationship with his daughter and his grandchildren, passed away in Los Angeles. I was thankful that at least we had fourteen years to try and

make up for all the years of being apart. I took the kids several times to the mainland for visits with him, and he was a proud grandfather.

I was fortunately healthy and strong, but for many years had not been happy in either of my marriages. I was always trying to make it better, but nothing ever worked. A battered wife, my marriages were a failure. I felt so alone; and when I tried to instill Jewish practices into the home, observing the Sabbath for example, or to tell the kids Bible stories about all the Jewish characters, I got resistance from Stanley. In later years, I recognized his behavior as Anti-Semitic. The third-time Stanley deserted us was the last. In 1988, we parted. I took the girls to start a new life in Scottsdale, Arizona.

ARIZONA

Imagine always being damp and moist from the environment and then going to a completely dry desert climate. The change was difficult and I had a hard time seeing the beauty of Arizona, especially Phoenix. My younger brother Warren came to the rescue and helped get me situated until I could get on my feet. Scottsdale was where we set up, in a rented house with some money to get by with for at least six months. I found work as a property manager with a prominent real estate company. Eventually, with all my experience and background I decided to put down roots and get my Arizona Real Estate License.

I was again a single mom and had to work in order to financially survive and support the girls. We lived in Scottsdale, part of the Phoenix area and were motivated to keep up with the neighbors. The girls went to Saguaro high school; and I worked at Ranch Realty, as their property manager, managing more than three hundred homes at both McCormick Ranch and Gainey Ranch. I could no longer spend hours in the kitchen making tofu, mayonnaise, or spaghetti sauces; instead I would buy things from a super market and put together fast meals. Moving to the 'mainland' was more of a culture shock than going from Nepal to Hawaii! Yet, even though I now had a dish-washer I hand washed the dishes and put them in the dishwasher to dry on the racks. I also insisted that each of the girls wash dishes as part of their chores. The apartment we lived in had a microwave that I refused to use, partly because I didn't know how to! The girls, though, pushed this and that button and figured out in an instant how to use the strange contraption.

SAYING GOODBYE

My mother was quite ill and was living in San Francisco. My older brother Mitchell then lived in Boston. He made the decision to have mother shipped out to Boston, and after many twists and turns managed to find her a suitable elder care home in Lynn, Massachusetts. He was close enough to visit and check up on her. She lived there for almost a year and seemed to be doing better than when she arrived. Suddenly one morning Mitch called and told me that I needed to come to Boston immediately, because our mother had suffered a complete body failure, was in a coma, and was not going to make it much longer. I remember that day very clearly: getting the call in the morning, and by 1pm taking a flight to Boston.

All her children (except the missing daughter) were gathered around her bedside. We all had our own memories of life with mom. One by one we had our moments alone with her. I sang, read, and talked to her; massaging our comatose mother made me feel close to her during those last moments. There was no struggle to communicate - she couldn't answer back, refuse to listen, or get mad at me! I felt as if I was comforting her, and was saying goodbye in my own way. There were many tubes attached to her; we all eventually agreed that it would probably be best for her not to be resuscitated if her body totally failed. It was a hard decision but it seemed that she was ready to go, and we didn't want her to suffer anymore. She passed away almost immediately after (almost) all her kids said goodbye!

After the simple Jewish funeral service, we talked over dinner about our life with our mother; a therapy session of sorts, it seemed to provide some sort of closure. I often think of our mother and truly hope her soul is at peace after all her years of torment and mental anguish.

ISRAEL

I did well at property management, but living in Scottsdale was growing on me. I was antsy and started feeling the urge for adventure, and to make one more travel jaunt; this time to visit Israel, the country of my ancestors. The years I'd spent in Hawaii living in a Christian atmosphere, and fighting to keep that symbolism out of my home, mightily contributed to my desire. At the Jewish Federation in Phoenix I asked about emigration but was told it would be better to first visit and then decide.

I saved money and just after the Gulf War joined a tour to Israel. The moment I landed at Ben Gurion airport I felt at home. I'd never felt that in any of the countries in which I'd lived, even after fifteen years in Hawaii. I toured the entire country. I would separate from the group, and wander into the local neighborhoods of Jerusalem, and into the Old City. People would come up and talk to me as if I were a local; but I couldn't understand or respond to them in Hebrew. I felt an outsider; even though Jewish. It became clear that this was where I needed to live out the rest of my life. I would return one day but not as a tourist. It took five years of preparation for the day when I would emigrate (make Aliyah) to Israel. The girls were growing up and would make their own decisions about where they wanted to live. If they chose to make a new life with me, then we would do it together. Sidra was the only one who came to Israel with me. I tried to talk her out of it because she had not visited; but she'd become enthusiastic upon my return. She looked at all the pictures I had taken and she got the bug. Neima went to college in Flagstaff and Gema returned to Maui to live with her dad.

GAINEY RANCH

In Arizona I'd received a call from the Director of the Gainey Ranch Community Association; they knew my reputation for good property management skills at Ranch Realty. They had an opening, and would I be interested in applying for the position of Administrator? Yes, I was and went in for an interview. Instead of filling out an application I was given a personality test to take home, rather than to fill out on the spot, which was the normal procedure for hiring new staff. I thought seriously about what was at stake: I could answer the questions to meet what I thought were their expectations; then I wouldn't be honest about who I truly was. Even if I got the job I would feel as if I'd gotten it under false pretenses. I chose to be truthful. I got a call asking me to come in for a second interview with Fred, the President of the Association, my heart was pounding. I didn't know what to expect; it was such a big step up for me; a girl from Brooklyn, raised in tenements and public housing and on public assistance. A hashish smuggler and hippie turned Property Manager!

I was warmly greeted and asked to take a seat. Fred let me know that the results of my personality test matched their expectations of the kind of person they were searching for, to fill the prominent position of Administrator who would manage more than one thousand homes and condominiums - and when could I start? I almost fell over but must have looked very calm because I said that I needed time to think and that I would get back to them by the next day with an answer. I was shown around the building and the lovely private office that came with the position. I drove out of the gated complex through the guard house, past multi-million dollar manicured properties, eighteen swimming pools, and several golf courses. I hardly believed that I, indeed, had this opportunity to make a better life for myself and for the girls. I accepted the position.

Over the next three and one-half years I spent as Administrator for Gainey Ranch I solidified my decision to emigrate to Israel. I would meet Israeli home owners, take Hebrew language classes, and now that I was improving my computer skills I continued the search for my sister. My last days in Arizona were emotional; and when Sid and I put all of our belongings into storage, and I sat on the carpet in our empty Scottsdale apartment with nothing but my purse, I was able to feel like I was releasing my future into the hands of God, with a new purpose in life. I hadn't a clue as to what would happen once I arrived in Israel. Yes, it was scary, but liberating at the same time. I was starting over again, and would finally get to live amongst my Jewish people and be part of Israeli culture. I would return to where I was meant to be. I would prove the *shaliach* (the Israeli representative who receives applications from people who want to immigrate to Israel) wrong; when I first handed in my application he said that, at age forty-nine I was too old to make it in Israel, I would never get a job and never learn the language. On that carpet in the empty apartment in Arizona I was about to begin another journey.

POLAND

During the last years my dad was living in Los Angeles, he lived with his lady friend, June. She was friendly, and European with a thick Polish accent, who loved my father till his dying day. We'd kept in touch over the years, after my dad passed away; and whenever in California I would visit June. She visited me in Arizona at Passover one year; we got along very well. June's brother, Ben, was quite elderly and lived in Poland; but he went to Israel every year accompanied by a caregiver. After June heard that I was making Aliyah to Israel, she graciously offered to pay my way from America to Poland; and she contacted her brother who was ninety-nine years old. He offered to pay my way from Poland to Israel, if I would agree to take him there to spend his final days.

Everything was in storage and it was a few weeks until my flight to Poland. I was living out of two duffle bags at a friend's house. Then I slipped two vertebral discs. The pain was so incredible and intense that I'd crawl on the floor, and couldn't stand upright, or sit in a chair. Both the flight to Poland and travel inside Poland was going to be strenuous and long; especially since I was slated to be the caregiver for a ninety-nine-year-old man!

Many Jews wish to die in the land of their forefathers, and it sounded like a task I could handle. Ben wrote back and forth frequently those last months in Arizona. I called him several times at his hotel in *Bielsko-Biala* in the south of Poland. His English was excellent because he had lived many years in America and was an American citizen. I would join him in Poland; he would pay for all my expenses, and then we would go to Israel together soon after I arrived; I would help set him up in Israel, make Aliyah, and then go on my way. I let him know that my elder brother, Mitchell, would be in Eastern Europe at the same time I would be in Poland, and that we would want to spend some time together, since we hadn't seen each other in a few years. Everything was agreed to; or was it? Slipped discs were causing me enormous pain. How was I going to handle the long flight, schlepping two large duffle bags? Thank God for chiropractors: ten visits to a highly-recommended chiropractor managed to get me off the floor and walking again.

BEN

I said my good-byes. The plan was for me to get to Israel, rent an apartment, and get settled before Sidra would join me. She'd saved her money and would send a shipping container with all our possessions that were in storage before coming. I took a flight to Los Angeles and said goodbye to June and got my ticket to Poland, where I would fulfill my commitment to take care of Ben until we got to Israel. The flight to Poland was long; I landed in Warsaw and got on a small plane to the south of Poland. A taxi was supposed to be waiting to drive me to the hotel where Ben resided. There was no taxi, and it was very cold. I was Jewish and in the land where millions of my people were gassed, slaughtered, and cremated because they were Jews.

Here I was, with only one thousand dollars to my name, not speaking Polish, and needing to travel quite a distance before sunset. I eventually rounded up someone who spoke some English. He got me into a cab for the two-hour ride to *Bielsko-Biala*.

Passing through villages and towns as the sun was setting, made me feel far away from home. In reality I didn't have a home; but I told myself that it would be okay; that everything would be better once I got to Ben's. We finally entered the small town of *Bielsko-Biala*; and after the driver asked directions to Ben's Hotel we drove there. Ben was expecting me, since I'd called from the small airport to let him know that I'd arrived and would be coming to *Bielsko-Biala* by cab. The front desk staff, who could barely speak English, asked me to have a seat and please wait. They were very nice and treated me courteously. About one half hour later an elderly, but strong looking gentleman with a cane walked in. Here was the man who would cause me cry out to God in desperation over the weeks to come.

Bielsko-Biala is on the southern edge of Poland, neighboring the Czech Republic. It's a small town known as Little Vienna. The architecture is picturesque and it's surrounded by mountains. During World War II the town was annexed to Germany, and its Jewish population shipped to Auschwitz-Birkenau.

Though ninety-nine years old Ben was in pretty good shape; except for needing a cane much of the time and requiring assistance with other needs. At first, he was cordial. We were escorted up to his small two rooms. There was only one bedroom and a sitting room, a large bathroom with tub and another, tiny bathroom with just a sink and toilet. I asked Ben where he took his meals, assuming that he ate in the dining room downstairs. No; he only ate there on special occasions. Then in the tiny bathroom, on the floor, he pointed out the hotplate, frying pan. and sauce pan with which I was expected to cook all our meals. I was appalled. I was back to jungle life but without the vegetation! This aspect of my chores was not mentioned in all of our correspondence and conversations. He showed me the bedroom where I could store my luggage and get comfortable. We sat down and talked after I got some things out, and was as pleasant as possible under the circumstances. There was a large sofa in the sitting room that opened to a bed, and a TV with satellite hookup. We talked about our plans to go to Israel; almost the first thing I reminded Ben of was that Mitchell was coming from Prague, and that we would tour a bit. He said he knew nothing of that and this was the first time he had heard about it! He was planning to go to a spa in the mountains for the elderly for a couple of weeks stay, and wanted to leave *Bielsko-Biala* as soon as possible. That first night on the very hard bed in the room next to Ben, I cried to myself thinking that I'd made a very big mistake. I doubted my strength and ability to handle the situation. I wanted out and fast. How could I have made such a bad choice?

Mitchell would arrive in two days and everything was set, I couldn't reach him to chicken out. It was November and extremely cold. I had just come from Scottsdale, Arizona. Fortunately, I'd bought a winter coat before I left thinking that perhaps I might need it; duh! I hadn't owned a winter coat since the bear in Amsterdam. Winter boots, warm leggings, and socks though did the trick. Ben was upset that I was leaving him only a couple of days after I'd arrived; that set the tone for the next couple of weeks.

It seemed as if I was the only one at the train station when I got there at 10:30 pm. I was there a few minutes before Mitch's train arrived, it was an eerie feeling. There I was bundled up in boots, scarf, and gloves, walking on the frozen snow. The starless night was dark; I had a strange sense of being transported back to similar nights when Jews would be herded into to this train station huddled together, before being shipped out to god knows where.

Freezing and waiting, the train approached. There Mitch was also bundled up. We ran towards each other and embraced. I was crying because I wanted him to take me away and escape from this place. Memories of the orphanage came back; I was a big girl now and still needed someone to rescue me. We talked and got into a cab and rode back to the hotel right away. I filled Mitch in on the situation. There was a room reserved for him just a few doors down. Next afternoon we said goodbye to Ben and took a bus to Krakow. We were to stay there three days, then I would return to Ben and Mitchell would be on his way to Ukraine. We found a room with big double beds in a nice, old hotel in Krakow. We would go to Auschwitz-Birkenau and visit the Nazi death camp.

A group of Germans on a shopping spree were also staying at the hotel. One of them had collected about five thousand dollars from friends in Germany to purchase Polish goods. Preparing to leave the hotel, a hullabaloo ensued when it was discovered that the money had been stolen! Mitch told the police when they came, that the night before, when I'd left our room to shower - the charming hotel had only communal washing facility - a woman opened the unlocked door to our room. When the skinny, fortyish bleached blonde saw Mitch she skedaddled. The hotel staff seemed totally uninterested, though, in either identifying or tracking down the thief, who seemed to have full run of the hotel! Anyhow, one of the group kindly invited us to join them on their bus. They'd planned a diversion from shopping; an entertaining side trip to Auschwitz close by!

AUSCHWITZ-BIRKENAU

The ride to Auschwitz-Birkenau would be one of the most disturbing experiences in both our lives; it was excruciating: our fellow passengers were joking, and laughing, and barely interested in the surrounding countryside. To top it all off, the driver of the bus had kitschy German schlock pop blaring all the way!

On either side of the narrow road, were scattered patches of stark, thin, white-barked trees. I couldn't help but imagine what the Jewish people must have experienced as they approached or escaped such forested areas. At last the bus entered the parking lot at the Auschwitz section of the twin camps, and everyone disembarked. Mitch and I immediately high-tailed it and got as far away as possible from the German shoppers on tour.

Auschwitz itself was not a death camp. It primarily housed political prisoners and prominent members of Polish and European society including aristocrats, intellectuals, artists, and priests. Auschwitz is a town. The camp is situated in a more rural part of the town with quaint brick homes. Upon entering one of the buildings, part of the camp museum you start to get the feel of what went on there. One building housed photos of Polish political prisoners the Nazis had killed. Behind huge glass windows we saw mountains of eyeglasses, shoes, clothing, eating utensils, and prosthetics. A sick feeling came over me but we continued on to the execution area outside the torture building near block 11. Many gypsies and others were exterminated along with the Jews. Inside one building were small rooms used for torture and even a tiny space into which prisoners were jammed, side by side, standing up; and would be in the dark room for days on end. Another building housed a couple of gas chambers. The Auschwitz camp grounds were well maintained, not what you would expect from a death camp. Auschwitz, though, is merely a teaser to the horror of Birkenau, the mother of all death camps. Leaving behind the cynical optimism of *"Arbeit Macht Frei"* - work shall set you free - in Auschwitz, we approached the main entrance to Birkenau.

A mile from Auschwitz is the death camp of Birkenau; spiritually, though, it's in another universe. Birkenau is about the size of downtown San Francisco; it was a veritable City of Death on European soil. Mile upon mile of wooden barracks warehoused people stacked three to four rows high, and four or more in each wooden bunk. The barracks were about sixty feet long with one small stove for heating in the middle; not much bigger than the one we had in our van.

Through the main entrance at Birkenau, where trains would deposit endless carloads of victims to the sounds of barking dogs, shouts from SS Officers, and Alma Rose's orchestra which would soothe the arriving victims with tunes from their respective homelands, Mitch and I stood on the platform in total silence. It was an overcast, wintry day without many visitors. Eyes closed I imagined screams and felt the horror which must have inhabited those ejected from the trains as they turned to face the crematoria. I stood on the open grassy field and stopped in my tracks as I heard the spirits of the blood crying out from the ground. My tears and sobs went on for what seemed like an eternity. My eyes cleared, though, to behold Mitchell clambering like a goat - he's a Capricorn - over the ruins of the mangled crematoria. The Germans, in their haste to flee oncoming Soviet troops, could not entirely remove the evidence of their methodically evil savagery. Mitch would later recount, half seriously, that it was atop the twisted iron rods and chunks of concrete that he gained sympathy for Holocaust deniers! There he was, he said, in Europe's City of Death, all the evidence was in plain sight; but how could it possibly be true? Although a fact, it was one which his rational mind could not possibly comprehend or accept.

When we finally left much later in the day to return by regular bus to Krakow, Mitch and I couldn't utter a word to each other. It must have been the next day when we finally started to have a real conversation about our experiences of the day before.

We spent the next day exploring the *Kazimierz* neighborhood of Krakow. The city's long gone Jewish community was centered there. We ate in a kosher restaurant in the once Jewish neighborhood. Poland by then had gone through a burst of philo-semitism. The Jews were long gone, so it was safe and acceptable for a wave of nostalgia to set in. The neighborhood had become almost a theme park of Judaica. There was even Yiddish Theater with no Jewish actors. We talked to one elderly local man who seemed to take a shine to us. He blurted out as we were about to take our leave that, as a Catholic boy during the Nazi occupation, he'd heard his parents and neighbors' express approval for the extermination of Poland's Jews by the Nazis: "they did it for us"!

Mitch put me on the bus to *Bielsko-Biala* and he was off to Ukraine. I returned to Ben at the *Magura* hotel. He was still unhappy with me for leaving him and going off with my brother. I reminded him that it had all been prearranged and that I'd written him several letters about it; he said that I never did; the silent treatment, anger, and then bullying reared its ugly head. Somehow, we managed to get through the next few days. I had the extremely unpleasant, almost nauseating task of cooking for us on the bathroom floor. I made very simple dishes as he directed and also some of my own. He enjoyed my cooking. Ben's hotel suite had a TV and we would watch BBC, and other news stations, for English language programs. Mostly available were programs dubbed into Polish.

On the evening news of November 4, 1995, the breaking news from Israel would cause a major problem for Ben and me. Yitzhak Rabin, the Prime Minister of Israel was assassinated in Tel Aviv, and the first words out of Ben's mouth were, "There'll be civil war, so we can't go to Israel now". I think it was a panic attack I experienced when he uttered those awful words. My sanity required I believe that the distress of staying in Poland with Ben would end soon and we would finally be off to Israel. I didn't know what to say, I had to choose my words carefully or he would misinterpret them to mean something else. I asked when he thought we might be leaving; he didn't know and was more concerned about getting to a mountain retreat.

We drove into the mountains to a health spa; with an ambience of the 1940s & 1950s. There were treatments for different types of ailments. Food was served in the dining rooms, but Ben insisted that I cook for us in our two-room suite. I had a little table in the salon area to use for that purpose. Thankfully, the bathroom served only as a bathroom! We stayed there for two weeks. It was more pleasant than being in *Bielsko-Biala*.

One night I lay in my bed and threatened God. I told Him that if by a certain date, we didn't go to Israel I would just leave and go by myself. That was it; I couldn't stand being around the nasty man for too much longer. Two things stood in my way of leaving though: I had given my passport to Ben when I arrived, because he said he needed it to purchase my ticket; the other was that my one thousand dollars were slowly but surely dwindling. The cost for a one-way ticket to Tel Aviv was about five hundred dollars; and that wouldn't leave me much to live on once I arrived.

After two weeks of spa treatments for Ben, we returned to Hotel *Magura* and cooking on the bathroom floor. Caring for an elderly person requires a lot of patience. It also depends on the elderly person's personality. Ben had a strong will and he was a bully. He would scream and yell to get his way; and was also obsessed with his bowel movements. If he didn't have them at least three times a day he would get upset and take something to make him evacuate his bowels. He was so impatient waiting for the treatment to take effect that sometimes he would have accidents in his pants. That could happen anywhere, and I was the cleaner and washer of his clothes! Once he wanted an enema; I bought a home kit and asked if I could administer it to him. I had given my kids enemas, but never an adult. Strangely, he wasn't embarrassed to have me give him an enema; but was embarrassed when I would clean his dentures, and he refused to have me look at him without the choppers in his mouth.

The first time we went to *Krakow* together was a nightmare; it was after we'd returned from the mountains. Even though Yitzhak Rabin had been assassinated, I strenuously urged him to fulfill the promised arrangement to go to Tel Aviv. I kept checking the weather and reminded him of all the sunshine we were missing out on. He relented and made a day trip to *Krakow*; to visit his bank, buy travelers checks, and check on flights to Tel Aviv. My passport was still in his possession. I'd thought many times to search for it, but then guilt came over me about going through his personal items; so, I tried to be patient, while simultaneously remembering the deadline I'd given god. Before we left the hotel, I reminded him to go to the bathroom so that he wouldn't have to go on the toilet-less bus to *Krakow*.

It was freezing, a winter day in Poland; not something anyone used to hot weather dreams of. Ben and I rode through the same country-side Mitch and I had traveled through weeks before. The small town of *Wadowice*, Ben told me, was where Pope John Paul II had been born. The bus came to a stop and picked up more passengers. All of a sudden Ben grabbed his cane and small bag, and started to get off the bus without saying a word to me. I called after him but he just made a beeline off the bus. I followed in cold pursuit. The bus pulled away on its continued route to *Krakow*. Old, swift Ben was already down the stairs of the station. I called out and heard a faint voice asking for toilet paper come from one of the freezing bathroom stalls. On the women's side, I payed for a bunch of toilet paper. I handed it to him under the stall and waited.

Finally, Ben emerged from the toilet, and we talked about what had just happened. I scolded him for leaving me on the bus without letting me know where he was going; it didn't seem to bother him that I could have wound up in *Krakow* by myself, wandering around without him. Two hours later the next bus came. There was no waiting room inside the building, only a stall outside in the wintery elements. It was *extremely* cold.

When the bus arrived, we made it to *Krakow* where Ben took care of his bank business. We got into a cab to the bus, and returned to *Bielsko-Biala* with no airline tickets, and not a hint that departure for Israel was going to happen anytime soon.

Five weeks passed for me in Poland and it got colder and colder. I was chilled to the bone all the time. My demanding prayers were answered just as I was ready to pack my things and leave. Ben had a change of heart and felt that it was now safe to travel to Israel; we got our tickets and would set out in two weeks' time. I was delighted to know that I would be getting out of Poland and enter my new home. The next two weeks were as challenging as the previous five weeks; I continued cooking on the bathroom floor, and washed all of Ben's clothes and mine in the bathtub by hand. I also entertained his guests, who would come over and challenge Ben to a game of chess. He always won. I served him herring and vodka every day. I shopped and tried to make friends with the local staff at the *Magura's* front desk.

I was curious one day about something that was posted on a marquee in the hotel lobby and wanted to know what it said. I asked Ben to translate for me but he refused. So while he was in the lobby, I went over to the front desk and asked one of the staff about what the sign said. They spoke only a bit of English and were happy to practice, by telling me about the event which was going to take place. Ben saw me talking to them. He came over and stood very close; raising his cane, as if about to strike me over the head! Yelling, he told me not to talk to the hotel staff or he would beat me. That was it. I had been a battered child and wife; there was no way I was going to take that from a nasty old man, even if he was fifty years older than me. I stood my ground, looked tough, and yelled right back at him that he was never, ever, to talk to me like that again. He better not raise any thing to me, especially his cane, or I would take it away. I demanded in front of everyone in the lobby that he give me back my passport, which he did later that day.

We continued to get ready for our journey to Tel Aviv. As the day approached I really tried to hold it together. We would watch TV and get into arguments all the time. Anything that I said, Ben would say the opposite; it was as if he was trying to get me to react and once I reacted, things would spiral out from there. One evening we were watching a BBC news report. A black woman broadcaster was speaking and Ben blurted out, "Black people's hair doesn't grow". I couldn't let that go by without saying, "No, that's not true, I know plenty of black people whose hair grows". Ben: "No they don't", you don't know what you're talking about, and you probably will marry a black person"! The conversations became more bizarre as the time to leave Poland got closer. Finally, I just kept my mouth shut to avoid a confrontation.

The day arrived to leave the Hotel *Magura*. We took a cab to the train station; I with two big duffle bags and Ben with his entire luggage. We were helped onto the train and set out for the long journey to Warsaw, where a relative of Ben met us at the station and got us to the airport. Once at the airport I experienced the worst of Ben's tantrums. We were at the ticket counter exhausted from the long train ride. At that point, it was easier for me to put Ben into a wheelchair and push him around. My passport and ticket were all in order, but something was not quite right with Ben's passport. He somehow had entered Poland without being issued an entry stamp; and therefore, he was not able to leave. He began ranting, raving, and carrying on. Ben yelled at everyone and raised Cain, literally! He made such a turbulent scene that after about an hour of the frenzied old man going off the deep end, the authorities stamped his passport and let him go through. I thought for sure that he would have a heart attack right there in the airport, because his face got all red and he was so furious and angry.

We waited for the plane to arrive and boarded without further incident; and, thankfully, our seats were separated. The connecting flight to Israel from Italy was not long; when we got there, something went wrong with the next leg of the flight. We ended up waiting five hours on the plane before taking off for Tel Aviv. Ben only had to use the toilet a couple of times during the long day. We landed in Tel Aviv at 10:30pm, another of Ben's relatives was there to meet us. We gathered our bags and he took us into Tel Aviv and to the Maxim hotel on the shores of the Mediterranean.

THE PROMISED LAND

Leaving the plane was like entering heaven. The atmosphere was what I had longed for. I was so happy to finally arrive at my long-awaited destination, my new home. What I'd thought would be just a couple of weeks from when I left the States, turned out to be seven of the longest weeks of my life. I had just completed what seemed like a triathlon, but still had one more test to endure. There was only five hundred dollars to my name.

We arrived late and didn't have reservations which I thought Ben, or his relative, would have made in advance. We waited a couple of hours for a room. That's right *a* room, a *tiny* room, that Ben and I would share for a week! I thought I would lose it at that point. I would be certain he was asleep in the queen size bed, we would share for the next week, before climbing in; Ben on his side and me on mine. There wasn't even enough room to put down a blanket on the floor for me to sleep, the room was that small. The beds were two joined singles, not enough room between them to separate so that we'd would have some distance between us. That was all the hotel offered us. That first night I changed out of my winter clothes, ran down to the sea, and was thankful and optimistic about what my future would be. I was so very thankful to finally return, at last, in the land of my ancestors.

The next morning, I made my way over to the Ministry which handled new immigrants, registered, and was told to come back in four weeks. After a week of enduring the tiny hotel room, Ben rented a furnished two-bedroom apartment a couple of blocks from the beach. I was in heaven! The apartment had a full kitchen, and a washing machine and dryer. I took Ben for several medical checkups and procedures during those four weeks we continued being together. I found a more than suitable replacement for me, a lovely, mature woman from Poland who spoke his language.

During those four weeks, I contacted a friend of a friend who happened to live a few blocks away from where we were staying; I'll never forget Ruti, who took me under her wing, and gave me an introduction into Israeli culture, and advice on what to do next. At the end of four weeks I went back to the Ministry as they had instructed. I was handed my Israeli ID and became an official citizen of Israel. It was a glorious day and I could almost taste my freedom; especially after informing Ben that my commitment was now fulfilled. I gave him two weeks' notice and told him that I would be moving to Jerusalem, and that the Polish woman would then be taking care of him. We argued that night and Ben told me to not wait two weeks but to leave immediately. I made sure, though, that the Polish woman was in place before packing my bags. I definitely wasn't going to leave on a guilt trip.

The next eight months were taken up with waiting and preparing for Sid to arrive. I had to secure a suitable place for us to live. Life was not easy but I still believe it was the best decision of my life to move to Israel.

The first few years in Jerusalem were eventful and dangerous. Sid and I went through *Ulpan* (Hebrew language school) and had near run-ins with suicide bombings too close for comfort. We both worked in the booming tourist industry until the bombings and intifada intensified. We made many friends and I would frequently travel to the States to visit Neima and Gema, and my first grandchild. I increasingly embraced my Jewish roots; learning more about the practices, and how to observe the Holy Days and Sabbath (*Shabbat*). I light *Shabbat* candles every Friday night and keep a kosher kitchen. I love living in a country where so many observe the Sabbath. I've embraced all the Jewish Holidays and especially love building the *Succah* on *Succot*; hosting *Chanukah* parties and having family over for the Passover Seder. The richness and depth of what everything symbolizes, has filled my soul.

Over the years many of my friends, heard numerous stories about my life; and about the adventures which never seem to end. I always got the same advice; "you should really write a book". There was a huge missing ingredient to this book which is the long-lost sister that our family only relatively recently learned about. I believed that one day I would find her or that she would search for us and find me.

SISTER QUEST

On a weekend get-away with my friend Miri, after telling stories about each other's lives, she strongly encouraged me to search for my sister. Now I had a computer and access to the internet. The World Wide Web was coming of age; and perhaps I too was coming of age. The knowledge was out there to mount a serious search. Miri suggested I read the autobiography of Barbara Walters. I read it with interest; but when I came to the part about Barbara's father's rival in the night club business, Jules Podell of the Copacabana, I had an incredible longing to pursue the connection. I contacted a friend in Arizona. Steve was a paralegal; he'd done some investigative work for me years ago, also in a preliminary search for my sister. Now it was different. I felt in my guts that this time my search would soon bear fruit. I hadn't felt as optimistic before. Steve found an archive newspaper obituary from 1973 that showed a picture of Jules Podell. The text said that he was survived by his wife Claudia, daughter Malda, and two grandchildren. I had it, my sister's name! Knowing my sister's name was all I needed to push on with renewed fervor to search out new electronic ways to find her.

Another computer savvy friend suggested I place an ad on an adoption bulletin board; which I did: "Looking for my sister, who was adopted by the owners of the Copacabana, Jules and Claudia Podell. Mother's birth name is Frances Goldberg. Please contact...." NBC Dateline contacted me via email a few days after placing the ad. I was increasingly taken with the idea that I would truly find her and soon. All my thoughts raced toward achieving that goal; it was difficult to concentrate on anything else. There had been many years of thinking about the mystery sister out there. Born two years apart, we shared the same mother. Where would Malda be and why had she been given that name?

NBC Dateline contacted me again and we also talked on the phone. I was asked for permission so that they could locate my sister, since they thought it was a good story. If they found her would I be willing to be united with her on TV? Of course, I would, but would she? What about her privacy, her life? Maybe she wouldn't want to be associated with me? Who was I anyway? Some shlump from the Flatbush slums raised on Welfare. Why would someone raised with the best of everything want me as their sister? Maybe my younger brother was right; why would we want to disturb her life? I, though, wanted to meet my sister no matter what she might think about me; it didn't matter at all. She was part of me, and this would be a dream fulfilled and a journey accomplished.

I gave Scott, from Dateline the green light to try and find her. I went for it, like I had for so many other things in my life. A couple of weeks later he contacted me but without results. He couldn't locate her. The timing at that point was extraordinary. I had planned a three-week trip to the States in order to visit my daughter Neima, mother of Dominic my first grandchild. I was between jobs and it was a good time to go. I told Scott that if he could find her while I was in the States that it would be wonderful; his deadline was almost up for the story and sadly said he wouldn't be able to complete the assignment; he had run out of time. He did, though, give me contact information for a lawyer with the Jules Podell foundation. I tried calling him before leaving for the States but there was no response.

I landed in New York a few days later and with a couple of hours' layover decided to try again to contact the lawyer from the Podell foundation. I got an answering machine. The message that I left was simple: I'm the sister of Malda Podell and I'm trying to contact her. I'll be in America for three weeks and here's my contact information; would you please pass it onto her. He never did!

After a couple of days in Arizona the phone rang at about 4 am; it was Sid calling from Israel. Her first words were, "Are you sitting down"? No! I was lying down, sleeping; but with foggy early morning clarity, I attempted to focus on what she was about to tell me. Sidra was checking my emails while I traveled; she received the following response to my online posting: "Hi, I read your posting on the adoption bulletin board and I am the daughter of your sister. My grandparents are Jules and Claudia Podell, please answer right away."

I had to hold myself down because this was thrilling news which potentially fulfilled my wildest dreams. Had the search finally ended? Had the posting positively found my sister? It was too good to be true; I had to keep calm and stay focused, even at 4am. The return address on the email was a Fox News address. Wait a minute; could this be another reporter merely trying to get a story, and set up a TV reunion? I had to be sure. I told Sid to write the following, "Thank you for your email, I don't want to get too excited so I think it would be best if you have your mom call me here in Arizona while I'm visiting. I have some important questions to ask her and I want to be sure that this is indeed my long-lost sister."

Sid wrote the email to Jama, Malda's eldest child who was a producer at Fox News; she answered almost immediately; and set up Malda's call to me at a certain time so we could talk. You can imagine how fast my heart beat and my head pounded. There were so many unanswered questions. I had to keep cool and find out for sure if it was she.

When I posted the ad on the bulletin board, I left out certain facts that only the true sister would know. She would have to fill in the blanks. What if she didn't have the answers? Then what?

I kept watching the clock to make sure it was the correct time. Neima and I played cribbage, and then the phone rang. I leaped out of the chair with a leap that had me almost bounce off the walls in anticipation. Answering the phone Neima said, "Okay, here she is!"

The voice I heard was husky and definitely East Coast, which was a good sign. I politely began with hello; and told her that I had two important questions to ask her in order to be certain that we were sisters. With trepidation I asked, "What year were you born?" She couldn't be younger than me or older than Mitch; she would have had to be born between our five-year age difference. "1945" was the perfect answer to the first question. Now question number two, "Do you know where you were born?" Responding without hesitation she said, "Sydenham Hospital in Manhattan!" I screamed, yelled, and jumped up and down. She was doing exactly the same thing on the other end. This was it, this was IT!! The search was over; my missing sister was finally found. We had been returned to each other. A true Homecoming. I couldn't believe it and neither could she. We must have sounded like two crazy women, yelling and screaming; so excited to finally be known to each other. Anyone who has lost someone and then found them would understand. We, though, had never known each other. This was better than all the drugs combined I'd ever taken. The exhilaration was stratospheric.

We talked for about an hour trying to sort things out. Malda, who calls herself Mickey, wanted to jump on a plane and immediately head to Arizona to see me. I thought the same thing but needed to spend time with my daughter and grandson, since I hadn't seen them for a couple of years.

Hold everything! This was a major family event that needed to be documented; all of us together to meet, greet, and get to know each other. That would mean coordinating a family reunion. We'd have to plan it carefully. I still had to visit my youngest daughter in Maine, and Mitch in Boston. Mickey and I talked every day on the phone over the next two weeks. I would discover things that answered some of my questions. I still hadn't seen a picture of her and she hadn't seen a picture of me. What did she look like?

After two weeks in Arizona I flew to Boston, and went up to Maine to visit Gema; then back down to Boston, where Mitch and I hopped into his car and, telling family stories all the way, headed to Manhattan where we would meet our long-lost sister and her family. Sidra flew in from Tel Aviv, toting pictures - of my childhood, journeys around the world to Hawaii, and of my hippie days. Warren would fly in from California; and Mickey's three children would be there to meet their new aunt, uncles, and cousin. Gema and Neima could not be there but would meet Mickey a few years later.

Mitch and I were getting closer to New York City, and the excitement of imminently meeting our sister in the next hour or so, was nail-bitingly intense. It reminded me of the time the two of us were in Coney Island. We went on the cyclone roller coaster and sat in the front seat. I must have been about eleven and hadn't experienced anything like it before. We were locked in the seat; I looked up and realized that I was about to do something scary. As we inched our way upwards toward the peak of the first hill, I said to my brother that I didn't want to be there, and he said just hang on to me and don't worry, it'll be fun. I grabbed his arm and held on tight, tightly, and tighter and as the car reached the summit and we rushed down over the ridge; in fear and desperation I buried my head in Mitch's arm and bit it, as my heart almost leaped out of my chest. I can't remember if Mitch screamed because he was also scared, or if his arm felt the bite. Such was the intense feeling of my anxiety as we got closer to the city and to our sister.

My brother and I had, all the way down from Boston, recounted stories of over fifty years of our lives, which we'd eventually and somehow share with our sister. We speculated about her life during those years: growing up in the limelight of the Copacabana, surrounded by celebrities: would she be able to relate to us? Maybe she would reject us because of our crazy-quilt backgrounds, and certainly unorthodox lifestyles?

We arrived at our destination on West 73rd Street in Manhattan, where we'd stay for the next four days; then made a quick phone call to the apartment of Jama,

Mickey's daughter, where we would spend the next few days telling each other our life stories. We'd all try and catch up, and figure out why our mother kept us three siblings together, but gave Mickey up for adoption.

Mitch and I still couldn't get over how we'd all found each other after more than a half century. How did it all come about that we even knew we had a sister? What an identity crisis I was experiencing, having been the middle child all of my fifty something years; and now to realize that I had to share that space with another was at first uncomfortable. Maybe Mickey would feel closer to one of my brothers than to me, and that would put me on the outside. How would the sibling dynamics play out with our new-found sister? Such childish thoughts ran through my adult brain; but the one constant thought was that I now had a sister.

GENESIS

The process of finding each other began many years ago in California. I was on a visit to San Francisco, after having lived in Hawaii for a few years. Mom and I were having lunch at a restaurant in the Fillmore district. I'd said something that upset her. That was not unusual since we could barely have a conversation for more than five minutes without having an argument. She was quite angry and said, "I have another daughter, and she's famous, and she loves me!" Hmm? I thought; that's an interesting way to say that I wasn't a daughter she loved, and would prefer to replace me with someone else.

I was uneasy, to say the least, but held my temper and thought, maybe she just blurted out something to hurt me? She never, ever said anything more about a mysterious sister who was famous that loved her. At the time, I was staying with my brother Warren in Tiburon. When I related what our mother had said, he thought it was another of her hallucinations or, at best, a good tactic to get me upset. I decided to delve deeper and check it out. Who would know if we indeed had a sister? Aunt Martha was the one!

The phone rings in Martha's apartment in Brooklyn: "Hi, Aunt Martha, hope that you're well; oh, by the way, I have a question. Do I have a sister?" There was an endless second or two of dead silence, then the hysterically panicked yelling in response, "Who told you? How did you find out?" So, began the quest for our missing sister that would occupy us for years. I intensively questioned Aunt Martha over the years, and discovered that she knew a lot of information I was never able to get out of mom.

MALDA

These are the facts: Frances Goldberg was twenty four in 1945, and lived in Brownsville, Brooklyn. She'd given birth to her son Mitchell two years earlier. Benjamin, his father, was away at war; and would return from the Pacific front to marry her, and father their daughter Suzanne in 1947. In between she got involved with "someone", the father of the first daughter, who was immediately given up at birth for adoption by Jules and Claudia Podell, of Copacabana fame.

How does one bottle up a secret like that for so many years. Unfortunately, our mother never got to meet her baby girl but Aunt Martha did. In fact, during the last days of Grandma Molly's life, she'd begged Aunt Martha and made her promise to find *The Missing Daughter*. What a task to place on Aunt Martha's shoulders, and then to pass away without knowing if the missing daughter would be found.

We embarked on the sister quest in the 1980s, without having a computer or enough money to hire a private detective. We checked the New York City area phone books for the family name of Podell. Mitch and I made phone calls; none of the Podells we called were related to our Podells. Then life happened as it usually does; and people get busy with kids and responsibilities and time goes by.

Mitch and I had quickly walked the ten, short, horizontal, north/south blocks of Manhattan from West 73rd street to West 83rd street. Jama and her husband Tom lived in the penthouse of a classic pre-war building. The doorman expected us; and directed us to the elevator and up to the top. We were full of anticipation. We'd finally get to meet our sister; and over the next four days, we'd get to know Mickey and her family. I looked at Mitch as we stood at the apartment door. The Missing Sister was standing on the other side, anxiously waiting for us to ring the bell. Could we believe it? Mitch was excited. He also realized that his little sister was now the second youngest instead of the only sister. We held each other's hand and rang the bell.

What seemed like the longest ten seconds ever, turned into a burst of tears and laughter when Mickey finally opened the door. We took our first look at each other, embraced, and couldn't help screaming.

After rounds of embraces, laughter, and jumping up and down, I finally let her go. Then Mitch got to hug his new sister. We both could hardly believe how much Mickey resembled her mother, much more than any of my brothers or myself. What a trip! Then we all hugged again. Sid had arrived a couple of hours before and joined in. There were Mickey's kids Ben, Jama, and later Danielle. Our younger brother Warren came in the next morning. Tom, Jama's husband, held a camcorder on us for the next four days from the moment their apartment door opened. We sat and looked at photos. Mickey wanted to know everything about her mom. We all had stories but the theme was the same; her main question was, "Why did she give me up and not keep us all together"? We realized over that week that some questions would probably never be answered.

I called Aunt Martha who had been bedridden for years with Parkinson's. Her mind was still clear, and when I said it was me she of course wanted to see me. I reminded her of our lost sister; and told our aunt that we had found her. She didn't quite get it at first. There was silence and I imagine that she might have been crying at the thought. We saved the last day for Aunt Martha; all nine of us went over to see her!

Before trekking to Flatbush Avenue in Brooklyn, though, we spent the entire time together with Mickey and family. At the playground and pond off Fifth Avenue in Central Park, Mickey's old stomping grounds, she said to Mitch, "This was my playground, where was yours?" "Playground" he says, "what playground?" Mickey heard about our old stomping grounds, far from the Alice in Wonderland idyll of Central Park. We went to

restaurants, drank egg creams, and ate rice pudding. We told many stories.

Mickey and I were walking together behind the family crew heading towards Central Park; sharing romantic escapades of our younger years. She threw out a famous name and then my Wilt Chamberlain episode got mixed in. We went back and forth like that, trying to outdo the other like sisters, young silly girls. Then Mickey says: "I had a very brief fling with.........!" "No way," say I, "that can't be, so did I!" We burst out laughing so hard, that everyone nearby stopped and stared. The flings with......, son of a famous TV personality, were about ten years apart but it was definitely the same person.

We four siblings had a good amount of time to talk to and listen to each other. Mickey's mannerisms resembled those of our mother so much that it took time to get used to. Warren had had the most vivid and recent childhood horror memories to deal with. Now he was in the presence of an older sister who eerily reminded him of his mommy dearest. That would take some getting used to.

My two brothers and I were very close; now we had to integrate Mickey into our threesome. We are a foursome now and I had to learn how to share. It's not easy to share at age fifty-four but I learned quickly. All I wanted was to be with Mickey; I remember feeling jealous at times, thinking that she was my sister but she was their sister too. At each restaurant in New York we visited we'd tell waiters our story of how we found each other, the cliff notes version of course. They all smiled at our happy faces, we glowed wherever we went. We took pictures and created lots of new memories; the most memorable of all was visiting Aunt Martha.

MARTHA

We packed ourselves into two cars and drove from Manhattan to Flatbush Avenue and Kings Highway where Aunt Martha had lived for over thirty years in the same funky, rundown apartment. There were about five locks on the door and a faded, peeling Chinese mural on the living room wall, a reminder of the way the place once was when she lived there with her second husband, Nat; namesake of her first husband, Nat! Martha had recently revealed to Mitch another lifelong secret; of how and why she came to marry the first Nat decades before.

Over the years, Mitch would come down from Boston to visit our aunt. Once, Martha, who had been bedridden for a number of years, asked him to come closer and listen carefully to what she had to say. In great distress, and almost sobbing, she said please find Sol; and tell him what really happened, and that I still love him and always have!

Martha and Solomon were an item in High School, they loved each other, were inseparable, and probably headed for marriage. Sol's mother was not as enthusiastic about the prospect of their marriage as were the young sweethearts. She managed to meet privately with Martha, and in no uncertain terms made it clear to her that Sol's family had plans for him to go to college and to not tie himself down with a girl from a poor family. Martha was devastated; and immediately, without explanation, broke with Sol; who could not believe that the love of his young life had for no reason, and suddenly, abandoned him! Martha had lost her moral compass; and on a double date with friends, acted on a dare to marry Nat. On the stormy night before her marriage on the rebound was to occur, Martha, in great anguish wandered aimlessly; suddenly a great bolt of lightning struck a tree directly in front of her; it was burned to a crisp and, uprooted, fell on its side! To our young and future aunt, it was a sure sign from God that her life would be ruined if she went ahead with the marriage. Distraught and inconsolable over the irretrievable loss of her darling Solomon, was it perhaps a suicidal impulse which had her go ahead with the marriage and along a path of moral ruination?

Her plastic covered couch of years ago had been replaced with a hospital bed; and that is where Martha lived for the remainder of her life until going into a nursing home six years later. She never wanted to, nor could barely, leave the apartment. I would visit her every time I passed through on a trip to Arizona from Tel Aviv. Aunt Martha had round the clock helpers; but the apartment had roaches and there were mice traps around. Chi-Chi was getting old, and every time Mitch visited he'd take the Chihuahua down to Dog Heaven and have her nails trimmed. When I visited, Chi-Chi got a bath in the tub.

The Jamaican ladies who took care of our aunt, never touched the dog, and Aunt Martha couldn't at that point reach down to pet her. We'd pick Chi-Chi up so Aunt Martha could see her up close and pet her. She always yelled at Chi-Chi; her way of showing affection? The little Chihuahua would lie under Martha's bed and guard her; or was she hiding? Each time I left Aunt Martha after a visit I'd cry and wonder when I would see her again. She would always say that she didn't think she would see me again and then she too would cry. Visiting Martha in her later years had always been emotional but this visit, with the nine of us, would prove to be a real tear jerker.

On the way, we remembered to stop off at Junior's and pick up Aunt Martha's favorite cheesecake. After we parked and walked across Kings Highway we stood downstairs at the entrance to our aunt's apartment building. Mickey hesitated and had to have a smoke. It was a hard moment for everyone, especially for her. Since none of the others in the group smoked, we all waited for Mickey to finish; then, in double shifts, went up to the fifth floor in the small elevator. It was so very odd to those of us who knew our mother that Mickey held her cigarette just like mom did; it was hard to avoid thinking that our mother was with us. Mickey resembles her in so many ways, and even has our mom's skin tone; but when we saw Mickey holding her cigarette in the same manner as our mother, that sent chills up our collective spine. The sight of us all descending upon Martha's apartment might have resembled a passing parade. Martha may not have ever had this much company at one time.

We knocked. The caregiver let us in; it seemed as if she was overwhelmed by so many people in the small one bedroom apartment at once. Aunt Martha couldn't see who was coming in the door; her only view for the last six years, since she'd been confined to her bed, had been out the window. Mitch was the first to give her a hug and kiss, then me, then Warren, who hadn't seen Aunt Martha for many years. She recognized all of us, and we reminded her that we had found the missing daughter and here she was.

Even though Aunt Martha almost constantly shook from the Parkinson's you could tell that she was nervous and scared to finally meet her long-lost niece. Around the bed and into view came Mickey. She leaned over the railings of the hospital bed and took Aunt Martha's hand and we all started to cry. The tears were automatic; no one had to say a word. One by one the others were introduced and Martha got to meet her grandnieces and grandnephew.

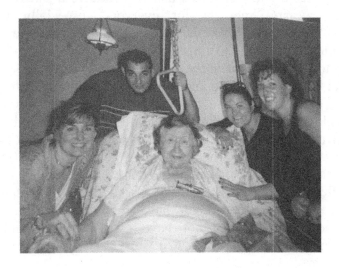

Sid came into view, and Aunt Martha remembered her from past photos. I think it was the happiest day of our aunt's life. She had had so much sorrow and disappointment and now she finally had something which was a blessing.

The most emotional moment of the visit, though, came when Aunt Martha turned her head to the wall. She cried out to her mother Molly and father Max's wedding photo hanging there, "I kept my promise to find her before I die". We learned that our Grandma Molly was heartbroken; that from fear of scandal she'd made her daughter, Frances, give up the baby; and that before our grandmother died, Martha was made to swear that she

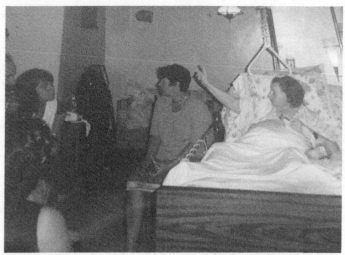

would seek out and find the missing daughter. That promise had now been fulfilled; and Molly's daughter was telling her mother, Mission Accomplished; we were all witnesses that she had been found! It was a heart-rending moment. Tissues were passed around the room a few times; and not a dry eye in sight for many a moment. Mickey had been found, we now all had each other - and we even liked each other! What a Homecoming.

Out came the cheesecake. With birthday candles lighted, we sang, "Happy Birthday to Us" and Aunt Martha wanted to know why? Our birthday party was in celebration of all the birthdays that we had missed as a family, and now we could celebrate all together. We talked with our aunt while Sid and Ben hunted through Aunt Martha's hoard of pictures.

They found some very old photos that none of us had ever seen; and even the original wedding invitation in  Yiddish of our grandparent's marriage in 1908!

It was hard to say goodbye. We all kissed and hugged Martha; and left not knowing if we would ever see her again. Back in Manhattan we began to process some of what had taken place over the last four days; a lot to take in and to try and understand. It wasn't only about me and my life, it was about Mitch's and Warren's and Mickey's life too. We live in different parts of the world but are family; no matter how far apart we're all together.

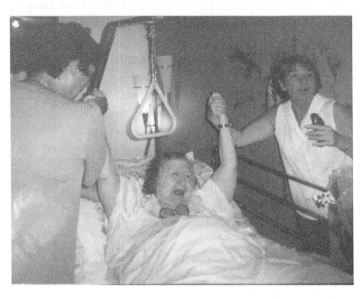

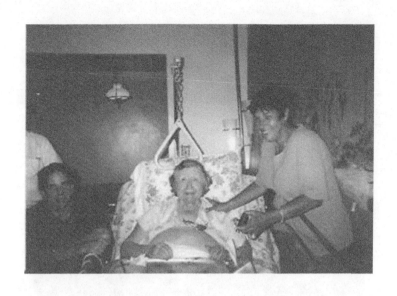

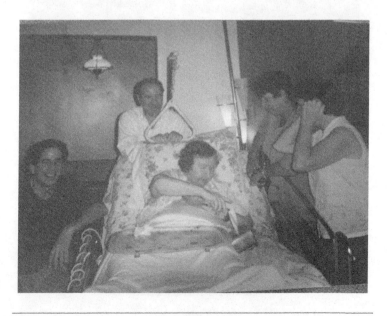

EPILOGUE

On my first birthday after finding Mickey, she sent me a book, "Sisters". On the first page, is the inscription: *To my One and Only Sister, Suzanne on her Birthday. I'm so glad you're my sister- you're just what I ordered. Every time I saw this book in a store, I smiled and thought how neat it would be to have a sister to give this to- Well my prayers have been answered.*

I treasure the book and my love for Mickey is as strong, or perhaps even stronger than if we had spent our whole lives together. I am forever grateful to God for the miracle of returning me to my sister and for her Homecoming. A year and a half later both Mickey and I had remarried, each for the third time. We met in New York with Mitch. In the hotel room Mickey and I couldn't sleep so we lay there talking. She said that it was sad that Mitch and I had all the memories of being together as children, and that she had none: "You guys must have memories, like pillow fights and all that fun stuff?" Hmm; Really?! I said; then got up, grabbed my pillow,

 and whacked her on the head with it! She couldn't believe that I actually did that to her. "This is war, so watch out!" Mickey grabbed her pillow, gave me a really good whack, and like sisters we decided to gang up on our sleeping brother. We pounced on him and woke him up with pillows flying all over the place.

Whack, whack, Mitch and I bellowed, "Here, you want memories"?! We screamed and yelled and thought that hotel security would tell us to keep it down; but no one showed up. It's so amazing to have a sister, I love her forever.

The Beginning

"This book will open your eyes about how children can survive the horrors of a childhood gone bad and survive against all odds. Seventy-two years ago, I was given up for adoption; my siblings weren't as fortunate. I was the second of 4 children we finally found each other after 55 years of lies and cover ups thanks to the Internet. It was a turning point in all of our lives. They all thought I was the lucky one because I had luxury surrounding me but all I wanted were answers to my heritage and a family to love. Over the years and developing a special closeness we discovered who the missing baby was. It was me. My sister tells a beautiful and truthful story about growing up her way. I know you will enjoy this book. I have."

Mickey

"As the song goes, "what a long, strange trip it's been". Being children without any real parenting, it always felt that we sort of raised ourselves. This tumultuous experience had us seeking our own separate futures as soon as were able, and at the same time brought us together as adults. I was just lucky to have had such a great and caring sister during all these years."

Warren

"Helping edit my sis's book, which recounts in vivid detail her life's extraordinary experiences, has brought me closer to her. I learned things, reading and discussing details about events in the long stretches of our lives apart as adults, which still surprise me. Her stories illuminate the crevices of character which make my sister who she is and our family what it is. As with odysseys since the time of Homer, artfully told adventuresome stories of distinctly personal experience can, paradoxically, echo the universal and thereby reflect and reveal both the heights and depths of human nature."

Mitch

Made in the USA
Coppell, TX
05 March 2021